CONTACT

AN ANTHOLOGY OF MODERN POETRY

Edited by

H. M. ROSENBERG

Idlewild

IDLEWILD PUBLISHING COMPANY
543 FREDERICK STREET
SAN FRANCISCO, CALIFORNIA

"Late Autumn" by *Robert Necker previously published
in* Saturday Review.

Only one thing to me is important:
That there be poets,
Many excellent, different poets!
   — Vladimir Mayakovsky

INDEX TO AUTHORS

TOM ADAMSON

FOR YOU TO SEE ME

Composition, my bliss.
Thought, a minted dew,
but images flow away
at the nearness of you.

I'll step on the foot of those tyrants
to bridge fromnever to forever.
We'll go down — down — down
down together.

AN AMERICAN DREAM

Sweep away
laughing times,
cracked ceilings
that didn't scream
at a gingerbread world
with garbage for to
color me.

And at my cottage
came a bird with two knocks
wrapped in a phrase, like —
there's a smile on the dying
sun, like — roses are to grow, like —
you can't quit, like — Jesus was
bugged, too.
Perspective, man, perspective.

Down deep under
I know everything was put on backwards
and I'm spinning back to where
the trees shade themselves
and pride is worn over your left-eye
so you can't see half the sin your in.
Yeah going home to suckle my cloud
wrapped in Medea's beacon,
I'm coming home.

1

PRAYER IN A DARK MORNING

Not dark shadows of talk,
  but nothing.

Not the cover of death,
  but nothing.

With revenge; "And I have seen
          and I understand
          You must see God
          with your hand."

Not from zero to hell,
  but nothing.

With superiority; "And I suffered
          and I have knelt
          but never alone
          for God has felt."

THE FRUIT

Blood, there was.
Bawling mouth of it,
And came the dawn of reality
And hope.

The thrill of life
was in the cloud of hope,
the kiss of the future was on
my lips.

And suddenly. *Knowledge.*
The chilly inviting death
of nonsense and it's courter —
God.

And now, the shade.
To cool my soul, I will sleep
with innocence — but it will be a
restless love.

Blood, there was.
Bawling mouth of it,
and came the dawn of reality
and death.

2

DEAD ROSES

The breath of the old folks
stirs the dead roses
and bends the shadow
over the old god
of armistice with them,
of hope in them,
as a new day
fingers its way
along the path.

Hanging out wet thoughts
to dry in the wind,
patterns erased,
and silk flies in praise
of man, the good, the great
one-armed holder
and protector of life,
smiles,
and dead roses.

UNFINISHED MELODY

Lines of love linger
where my eyes your heart to finger,
to sweep the notes to sing.

Icebergs to tears may form
notes we say will not fly the warm
sun in the dark, love is the thing.

THOMAS A. ALFANO

OF MY LOVE (POSTMORTEM)

I'd found my dear eternal flame.
Made bliss my plight and by the same
Quenched I by light drowned was night's sorrow
Lit paths to view a dear missed morrow.

I'd seen her grow to bud to bloom
To touch her hand possessed the moon
But burning fires dwindle soon
As dying dawns incarnate noons.

THE REAPER

He whisks across vast grey deserts
   high on laughing wings of woe.
He chills the very spring of nature;
   bleeding wounds of wind, saps flow.
Through pale valleys to grey deserts.
   Sets he down to rest and drink.

Shrouded fleshless soul of torture
   forges raged torrents to below,
Waning springs the few who greet him
   onto cool green meadows flow,
Springs — torrents, flowing, greying.
   Waiting now with gnashing teeth.

EDMUND D. ASSANTE

SWAN SONG

Softly and slowly she gathers 'round her
Softer folds a white silk slip
Summoned to enfold font of softest down;
Along lingering, cygneous waves
A crest of tender press, and tenderer release.
Each dimpled pinch and phase recall
In a flash of pink all circumfused
The sound within — a polyphony
Of epithalmic symmetry.
The swoon of sweet mellifluous mood
Muting soft white mist of bugled passion
Spent in a silken cithara of sleep.

LETHA BALDWIN

INSPIRED BY TRANSFERRED ELECTRONS

Shirts thrown from the window explode so noisily.
Death is always untimely and skirts are short.
The window-pane is lovely.
Can the chain hold?
Men fight with fists and fall into the water.
Skirts are very short.
When television shows are funny a viewer should always laugh.
When rum makes a gold tooth sensitive, hunger lingers on,
But who will win the case?

4

Malicious toys will kill intruders too.
Wax must be scraped off.
Tear a doll apart and it will make a noise. Ah well.
Skirts are very short.

A man must jump to miss the epeé.
And women dance and sing to be seductive,
While matadors steal wives of other men.
Cowboys ride and shoot,
And clowns wear foolish clothes to make folks laugh.
A man is drowning in the horse trough now.
A raspy voice is saying silly things.
Horses sweat and strain
And desert flowers sell at half the price.

BETH BANOFF

NOT IN VAIN

I have heard philosophers decry
The futile lowness of this mortal shoal,
As, by pointing out the dregs, they try
To show how cheap and bitter be the whole.

Crying, "Shipwreck!" from an airtight hold
Who despair the course but never man the bridge
Like hikers who before their paths unfold
Are sure the trail can never reach the ridge.

And I must grant: cathedral shadows fall
On beggars, liars, scoundrels, thieves, and worse,
And he who strides today so proud and tall
Must make his final journey in a hearse.

But, too, each spire that seeks to pierce the sky
Was built by little men, who dared to try.

THE SNOWS LIE DEEP

The snows lie deep on the trampled ground
Where recent cannon thundered and bullets whined
And the warm air reaked of the bloodthirsty sound
And living men marched through the jaws of time.

Now shadows of headstones fall across the snow:
White purity blown by the winds of fate
Lining the hills where one was camped the foe
Ere that oft etched and unforgotten date.

Their sons, and ours, watched the banners fly,
Shivered in the trenches, their destiny sealed,
Measured men's manhood by the deaths they die
And left their posthumous children to glean others' fields.

Now bloodied victims of hate's perfidy
Can share the peaceful snows of eternity.

PAULA BARNES

THE JADE

Autumn is a willful jade
Clad in tatters rudely made
Of colors red and gold and brown
Torn from Summer's discarded gown.

She taunts Summer with brazen face,
Subduing her in dry embrace.
Then Winter comes in silver lace,
Exposing harsh and frosty face.
She takes the Autumn jade by arm
And chains her firm from icy harm.

PEACE

I like to fish for trout
Along a crystal stream.
There to rout my troubles out
In sweet fir-scented dream.

DISSENT

The "Boys" die for my right to dissent,
But what would be their comment
About my telling others not to go,
When they die for my privilege to do so?

6

YOU DIDN'T HEAR MY CRY

You didn't hear my cry.
At first, it was but a sigh,
Wistfully pleading, imploring,
Tentatively exploring,
Seeking human understanding,
Quietly asking, not demanding.
But you didn't hear my sigh.
So my cry became loud
In shout and crowd,
More intensely insistent,
More blatantly persistent.
Now you hear the crackle of the fire,
Hot in misery's savage ire.

Now you hear my cry.
Stand or die!

THE MEN IN BLACK

The men in black sit high and dry
In sacred Ivory Tower,
Making rules with which we must comply.

And not within the realm of doubt,
Some of their edicts are not without
The seeds of our dissolution,
If we keep on in their execution.

SHRIVE PAUL BECK

THE CITY OF THE DEAD

Pictures on the wall
A radio turned on
Shouts mingling in all corners
Chasing out silence and thought
There is a brief struggle,
Then the noise prevails.
Laughter . . .
Tears . . .
Deafening solitude,
Separate cubicles of excommunication
Confusing . . .
Strange
A world full of wireless telephone booths
With locked glass doors
Shades drawn.

TOMM BELZ

NOEXIT, A PLAY

(the september sun settles
in the bluish tint of the
horizon.
a feeling of love is felt
throughout the fibers of
maple leaves.
a rather youthful girl(
mysticized by her beauty
and newly found grace)
walks up to the front of
the stage and recites:)

mao's mother was a mobster,

sinful sex is sorrowfully secure.

(and then meditates:)

cats feet . . .
rubbing against the
    newly laid pavement.
i feel it,
    it must be real;
and (since) life is
only once, and one&only,
i must enjoy it to the
    fullest . . .

(blue lights are flashed
onto her face, as she smiles
and whispers to the
audience:)

security is just a word

    (please applaud,
        and leave quickly)

```
            )THE FLOWER
        the
         ch
              i
         l
         d,

            cries

              i

         n(

            the

         e(rather)

          m
        pty

          h
           a
        ll
        s       .

                  *

        )the flower has died

        ASCEND THE STAIRS
    ascend the stairs and look in,
                  (it's only me);
           t
             a ke

                  an

              i

                  n
    w
       ard

           look

              it's only you

                      .

                  .
                      .

                  .
                       .
        let's take

                  a      trip  .
                    9
```

AUDREY PEYTON BLACKBURN

FOG

A lovely gray blanket
Of nothingness appears
On the landscape. It
Looks soft and inviting,
Beckoning one to venture
Into its dark mystery
And explore the crevices
Of its velvety folds.
On stepping into this
Appealing world of fantasy
One is greeted by a clammy,
Wet, spider-web
Veil of sticky, clinging
Dampness. The moisture
Seeps into one's bones
And chills to the marrow.
The lovely world of fantastic
Mystery disappears with
The cold starkness of
Reality.

BARBARA DRATLER BLUM

WHEN AUGUST MEETS WITH SWEET SEPTEMBER

When August meets with sweet September
Promises of Autumn come.
The days (as does a dying ember
Boast when blaze and it were one)
Crackle and sparkle with transient heat
That'll soon disperse in breezes sweet.

The ripened, swollen, acorns, chestnuts,
Savored hungrily by squirrels
Will deck the roads with shells of best nuts
Clothe the streets in amber pearls.
But some nuts snuggle and sleep below
While patiently they await the snow.

The trees now shed their warm and flaming
Coats of leaves with haughty pride.
It's Winter they are aimed at shaming
Naked, bare, her cold they'll chide,
While a sea of leaves flutters, and flows
Chiding cold Winter's coloress snows.

10

MARTHA BRADFORD

HE DOESN'T KNOCK

Have you ever met my little friend?

You haven't if you've ever smiled, 'cause he doesn't
make people glow. He doesn't knock when he comes to
visit. Sometimes you can't call him by name, but
you know he's there.

Have you met my friend?

You have if you've been in a room with people and
had the feeling that you were standing on the sand
overlooking a large empty ocean. You've seen
my friend if you've felt small crystal drops slowly
glide down your cheeks.

Have you seen my little friend?

You have if you've watched a clock slowly tick late
at night and wondered why the hands seemed to cease
moving.

You'd know him if you had stopped in a graveyard
on top of a hill and watched the wind toss the
grass to and fro and knelt by a stone and cried
out to someone, but only heard the wind.

Have you met my friend:

he's sort of a strange fellow, sort of cold and
aloof, but you'd know him . . . well, almost
as well as I,

But never quite as well.

ARTHUR BRADLEY

He pleaded mildly for a kiss,
And thought "No good will come of this;
She stirs hearts as I stir tea,
And romance shows the clown in me."

11

He had a gift, as you'd suspect:
Intelligence in retrospect —
But when a thrill competes with sense,
The wisest are completely dense.

With sultry poses, sexy glances,
The wench provoked his crude advances.
He started somewhere near the middle,
Like a cheetah on the fiddle.

With passion less, confusion greater
(Brazen nymph and timid satyr)
He struggled to sustain the mood —
Alas! He had no aptitude!

Above, from Heaven's open portal,
The disenchanted Greek Immortal,
Venus, turned back from the scene,
And yielded to Saint Augustine.

JESSIE C. BROADFOOT

HURRICANE

Gangrenous vapors softly cry
The coming of the sickly sigh.
Flashing scalpel blinds the pain
Of cancer in the sewer gas rain.
Schizophrenic hurling sheets
On the cobbled, bloody streets.
Shocking, rocking, shaking, quaking
Then convulsive, bandaged aching.
Sonic boomings mark completion,
Scattered pulses expiration.
Sap smells shroud the fever's plunder.
Nuded willow blushes blunder.
Sterile patter douches wound.
Desecration breaks the gloom.
And the charnel-houses send
Those they bury back again.
Air, earth, water, fire
Sweating surgeons now conspire.
Diagnosis blown insane
Once again, the hurricane.

12

Standing with the pot of geraniums
In her hands
A clay pot with one red flower blooming
In her freckled hands
Standing there by the polished, speckled stone
With the moldy lichen crumbling
Standing in a faded cotton dress
A shirtwaist with a bit of ric-rac
Dangling from the worn sleeve
Standing by a grave at noon
In the cloudless sunlight
Without a shadow.

faintly sighing spider's winglet
floating in your obscure nearness
luminescence of this stillness
all around you zigzag straightness
softly do I look upon you
cradled in your own mind's spiral
let us dance to rhythmic silence

Not that ghastly slit-eyed wailing!
Barely shrouded by my fearing
Is the snoring of a tree-squirrel
(That moronic state of being)
Which is whirring, purring, singing
On the pine bough loosely twitching
Shadow skyhook in this limbo
Let us rumba like the willow

STEWART M. BROWN

NONLOVE

This is no time to study.
There is a world outside that window.
No, not outside the window that shows the paling blue of a dead
    day and beckons the ribaldry of night.
It is outside the closed window, drawn shade, and closed door
    of the student's mind.
We sit at the 100% pure ethnic desk cluttered with half written
    papers and cigarette stubs and close our minds to a world
    of reality.
We date 100% pure ethnic University girls with their false sense
    of morality and super sophisticated talk, so completely
    inane, of lofty metaphysics.
We hold bull sessions in our 100% ethnic rooms and brag about
    what we haven't done on dates or tell crude jokes.
God pity the miserable bastards who came to the University.

THE NOTE TAKERS

An old room in an old building,
Dirty walls,
 Bare pipes,
  Rough desks
   And worn wood floor.
The prof. talks on as students nod.
His voice drones on
Because he is an expert
And knows all in his field.
He mentions a date and 150 pencils scribble
He tells a dumb joke from 7th grade and the brown nosers laugh.
With only 6 hours of sleep it is hard
To Listen
 Not to nod
  To take notes
   Not to sleep.
The boys look out of the corner of their eyes at girls
Who pretend not to see the boys looking at them.
There are two kinds of girl on this earth
½ of them
 Wear no makeup
   Have long straight hair
     Wear wheat jeans
   Wear sweatshirts
 Wear tennis shoes and no socks.
The other ½
 Wear makeup
   Curl their hair in a pageboy, flip, or beehive
 Wear dresses
   Wear stockings and medium heels.
But in the beginning they are all alike.
Did I tell you who called . . .
Did you hear what Linda . . .
Well I heard . . .
And the gossip flows like blood from the fresh wounds in backs.
One of the nameless backs lights a cigarette
And I wonder how high the smoke will drift before it disappears.
Three other people act fidgety.
The pendulum doesn't swing,
The sand doesn't fall through the pin pricked hole.
The voice drones on,
The pencils scribble,
The heads nod,
And life drones on.

FLIGHT

Impatient businessmen bragging and drinking
Reluctant mothers tugging at reluctant children
Brothers of 5 holding onto sisters of 4.
Everyone talking
Mad travelers at wrong windows
Pleasant music that gives headaches and spotless hard floors.
"Flight 509 is boarding."
Brief scurries and a long line
"Your ticket please."
Out of the music clean room and the cliche counters into the
        outside.
The rain is just enough to be cold and noticeable
A 1000 ton metal shapeless form, with a deep gaping wound in
        its side
People of all kinds pour lustily into the wound.
"Welcome aboard flight 509."
Seats by the window are gone.
A strange seat and a strange face.
"Is this seat taken?"
A new confidant
The young tell all to their dearest friend of five minutes
I am from how nice oh yes no yes yes Johnson Kennedy Acron boat.
Ugly faces press against too small round windows and the children
        wave goodby to those who have already gone home.
The plane hums for ten minutes.
The door is shut.
A strange quiet is everywhere and I marvel at the acoustics.
The plane vibrates and propellers turn.
Smoke is spewed back over the tin wings.
"Good afternoon, this is your stewardess Miss Blah."
"Please fasten your safety belts and don't."
The plane turns and rolls bumpily down to one end of the runway
        where it turns into the wind.
There is lots of noise now,
Air conditioners coughs laughs all artificial and mechanical.
The left wing roars like an approaching freight train as the
        clumsy eagle turns.
Each motor is tested so that when we lose three engines we can
        land safely
And have our story in the paper.
The engines quiet down and we roll.
They roar and we are pressed back in our seats by the pressure
We're up, down up down

15

A highway pases beneath us.
We're up.
Over highways and cars and telephone poles houses churches
The plane still vibrates and the town city country is below us.
The pressure changes and we are glad Miss Blah gave us gum.
"Daddy, Daddy I wanna didja Looky mommy."
"Dinner will be served at no o'clock."
There is enough noise that when one shuts his eyes he is in
        his own world
Hemmed in by thin sheet metal and the roaring of engines.
"Would you like? May I get you?"
Miss Blah repeats her broken record for everybody.
For all those smug monkeys in their paper shells
Miss Blah must be cotton candy to all these hairy apes
Egocentric nuclei of small worlds.
She puts up the small table for those healthy men who were
        football stars
A wisp of her hair falls down and I find it pathetic.
The plane bumps & joggles its way through the silent gray world.
A graceful soaring animal.
No wound now, but grace.
People on the aisles read
People by the window blow mist on it through their filthy noses.

JOHN BURNETT

From dust to dust and ash to ash,
Thusly goes the peace into some war-trash.
Stop the war? Have you lost your sanity?
We kill in the name of humanity!

Aggression to aggression and death to death,
A thousand men drew their last breath.
Stop the war? Have you lost your sanity?
We kill in the name of humanity!

Today a hundred thousand were slew,
Tomorrow it will be six million jew.
Stop the war? Have you lost your sanity?
We kill in the name of humanity!

Europe to Asia and then back home,
Millions of children, hopeless roam.
Stop the war? Have you lost your sanity?
We kill . . .

16

OBLIGATIONS

You owe me, the chorus rang,
Loud and long and strident.
Not only Joe and Jim and Annabelle,
But church and school and government.
And also then, a minor plaint,
You owe your long dead forebears.
And also all the helpless ones.
You must help all your brothers.

So, far from well and far from fat,
I set upon a journey,
To either justify their claims,
Or declare myself insolvent.
First I met Tolerable Jones,
Most likable and harmless.
"O ho," he said, "what a joke,"
"I am a creditor."

So then I looked up Stingy Smith,
Who owned our blessed mortage.
Mr. Smith politely said,
"You must be misinformed.
So many dollars you owe me,
Beyond that I know nothing."

And so for schools and government,
Their tallies were depressing.
But added up, I still could see
No sign of grim disaster.
What is my debt, I asked a man,
Well versed in matters social.
Your debt is this, he calmly said,
And pointed to his family,
And to his crest and to his name,
And to their reputation.
"What nonsense this," I primly said.
"Where is the final tally?"
He shook his head and turned away.

17

Finally, to end the quest,
A mountain sage I sought.
He looked into the fire long,
And finally broke silence.
"Your debt is paid," he slowly said,
"When you have added all you can
To all you have been given."
And then his voice rose loud and clear,
In frenzied exultation.
"And those who would do otherwise
Create their own damnation!"

REX CHAMP

on the ship i met
a lonesome man from siam,
who said i was just
dull and a bit of a snob . . .
how long he remained lonesome.

TOHN CHAYNE

FANTASTIC ANON

It seems to me, the rafters are hung —
With strange dreams that haunt me still!
And why is the earth — caught with a silence,
Pulling me onward until . . .
I'm lost in a maze of distorted shadows,
Creating a fear, without form.
Quelling a lust. A fever. A want —
But needing a moment that's warm.
I'm lost, it's true. But who isn't lost?
Don't question me. What of you?
Retrace our steps and weigh up our life,
Just how many dreams came true?
Re-live our lives — fathom the depths —
Plagues with a wish, yet, until . . .
We reach the moment to wonder with . . . why?
And the earth holds a silence — still!

18

THE TREE

I am the tree!
The forgotten tree —
Lost by time and man's memory.
In the beginning, I came from the earth
and the quiet dust, that gave me birth
and nursed
Me . . . to maturity.
Tall and free
But a wanting tree.

And it came to pass,
One day they came with the ax
And they saw —
The pride of me, without a flaw.
I heard the metal sing
And felt the sting
Of heavy blow,
Then trembling, I fell
to the earth below.

Chopped, cut, hewn and scraped,
Oiled and treated and molded to shape!
But what remained was without loss.
I became a stark symbol! . . . A towering cross!

With the nails embedded, the blood went free,
While time counted the hours of agony.
Without thoughts, without eyes — Yet, I was seeing
that I held the form of the Infinite Being! —

I stood beneath a wrathful sky
and as I held him, I watched him die —
Amid the wails of the mourners' cry!

Held by the earth whence I came,
But I knew no honor, no glory, no fame.
The world only gave me —
Perpetual shame.

A MUTED MAGIC

Hush!
Be still, my love.
I have no moon large enough to bring
    and nightingales escape me . . .
(I hear their flight of wings)
    and something . . . or someone with arrogance —
    disturbs this thing
    called spring.

But! You and I,
    in this wonderland, with breathless still of
    night.
Holding a stem of stars,
    on a candelabra of sighs,
    and ecstasy . . . (or by another name — delight)
We move, tenderly.
Holding hands with understanding, contentedly . . .
Warmed by the mystery.

And if the shadows be purple.
Let them be purple, closely knitted into the scheme
    for they only paint for us —
A rainbow of soft, velvet dreams.
    and if you whisper,
    whisper low . . . like a dove.
But, above all —
Hush!
    and be still, my love.

Let this love be a pleasing thing to remember,
When a faded spring hides in a lonely
November.

BARRY D. COHEN

    The body decays to powder,
windblown grains of man
cast upon forgotten shores.
    Bizarre shadows dance
in the dusk of undiscovered suns.
    The stardust wanders
throughout the Universe.
    The breathless dust pervades the All,
and life is born from the dust
beyond the stargazer's ken.

JOHN COLLIER

YOUTH

In bang out bang
From a mother's mouth
In a summer cottage
In a summer month
Describing her son
How he came in
And how he went out
And louder still
As summer went on
And finally ended
Summer was gone
In bang out bang.

ARK FLOAT, PEOPLE THINK, RELIGION SINK

Noah had a floating thing
Hark the bells
No hear No ring
Bible says a floating thing
Watch the water
No see no thing
Great in story a floating thing
Watch the people
No see, no thing
Ark in story, Ark in life
Different story, different life
Bible say, so and so
Ark float, people sink
People born, people think.

BAREFOOT

10,000 die each day it is said
Lack of food
Cold stone dead

Have many children, the church has said
The more the merrier
Cold stone dead

Millstone round poorman's head
Slice it thinner
Cold stone dead

Mostly people, not the church
Have many children, Cold stone dead

ANNE CORBIN

THE BEACH

I saw
The daisy
Growing
In the sand

The planes above
Roared
The motorcycles
Screamed

And lovers
Rubbed
Each other
In tender places

I saw
The daisy

TO A CHILD

Come to me
And
I will dry your tears.

Nestle in
The
Hollow of my arm.

Sit with me
And
We will laugh together.

I will tell
You stories
You have never heard before!

22

MOTHER

Mother,
Laughter in my life,
Sunlight in my day.

Where is the sunlight now?
The laughter that I hear no more
Is now a treasured memory
That comforts me
When no one smiles.

Mother,
Laughter in my life,
Cherished memory,
Warmth that I feel
From within,
Gaiety that is recalled
To turn the somber hour
Into a special holiday.

SUBURBIA

In this congested place
I hurry to some unknown destination
Caught up in frenzied haste.
When normal tensions slacken,
I create my own.

How can I sit when none around me sit?
How can I meditate when none are meditating?

I meet each situation with apologetic manner
A moment late, a day, a week, or more.
Each task that's done
Leaves many tasks undone.

When death arrives,
I'll be on time.

THOMAS F. CORCORAN

BEAUTY BASE TWELVE IN A DECIMAL SET

1

kronos winds, kroma spills,
the greeks earn their pay
in pedestrian arts.

union organizers
try to get their way
because strength in number

will guarantee the work
within the limiting
scales of colors of time.

2

four brothers and sisters
dance and walk and run through
the time clocks on the wall

and the union boss knows
what work has been finished
or remains to be killed.

in striving for status
each employee thinks his
color pay check is best

3

but flight remains equal
whether red, green or blue
because of deductions.

soon they will be changing
all the notes to white, or
black, i can't remember.

up-higher management
hopes that the greeks will not
become displeased with work.

E. H. COWLES

WITNESS A MORNING

No gull's wing
     caught
The rising sun
As the dark yellow
     rays
Struck this bare-rock
     coast.
Offshore, yellow-green,
     the sea
Throws itself against
     the stone,
As if to bring down,
     forever,
Those monoliths thrust
     up,
From earth-core,
     in adoration
For the elemental
     trinity
Of their birth:
     fire, air,
And
     water.
Red-rimmed
     eyes
Perceive the
     earth
As it must have
     been
When life first
     transcended
The sea.
Witness here the
     sun,
As it was when we
     escaped
The salt matrix
     and made
This beachhead on these
     rocks
By mere threads of
     life-ness.
Witness here a

morning,
Much like our
beginning,
As we drive
on,
From Bangor to
New York,
Through the sulphurous
fog.

INTERSTATE WEST

Delicate flesh-pink
fingers
Of cloud caress
the horizon.
Sunlight clings to
the edges
Of earth delaying
departure.
The machine and I
move,
On frictions of
fabric,
Transfixing the distance,
westward,
In mediums of speed
and time.
Darkness reduces landscapes
to shadow,
As miles lapse into
minutes.
Vision is limited to
the beam
Of machine-light,
and
Black windows
confine
The spirit of
movement
Within the steel frame
of transportation.
A mobile chrysalis,
I
Follow the sun —
westward.

WINTER WOODS

The squirrel's eye
    watches,
In the deafening
    rustle
Of wind and branch
    against
The human-fear
Of my intrusion.

Wind nullifies
    the sound
Of footsteps
    between
The trees of watchful
    eyes.

Identity is lost,
To an elemental
    scourge,
In the step-silent
    tedium
Of these gray
    hours.

I have become like
    a fallen leaf:
Blown, with dry
    raspings,
Across the
    carrion
Of other deceased
    seasons.

THE FIRST OF DECEMBER

7 a.m.
I turn from the window,
    leaving
The thought of frost
    outside
On the grass:
    orange-brown,
In the slanting sun-ray,
    and
Deep, morning shadow.

27

Cold glass surrounds
        the warm,
Moist spot my breath
        has left.
Slowly the breath-spot
        expires
In the penetrating
        cold.
The vista becomes
        clear.

Leaving the harsh
        landscape,
I return to my
        room:
Closing my door
        against
The temperate inconsistencies
        of the sphere.

LOCH CRANE, JR.

THE WINDOW ON THE SEA

The Sun is dead now you know
I know because I saw it die
It writhed and shone and burned as mightily as
    nature had permitted it to   for a few
    seconds   and then a gray cloud came and
    swallowed it and masticated as it passed before
    my window
Masticated and chewed and ground at the Sun as
    though it had bitten off more than it could chew
The Sun is a large bite you know

And now the cloud is writhing
Not mightily as the Sun did and not with as much
    energy but writhing anyway
It too fought and tried to avoid the inevitable
But it was mightier than the Sun   which was
    proved by the fact that it swallowed it

The cloud is ragged and grubby and a dirty dirty
    gray which makes it a shame that it swallowed
    the Sun
The Sun was bright and warm and young
And this old cloud was filthy dirty
Why does dirt seem to overcome beauty instead of
    beauty overcoming dirt

The cloud is thirsty now after its hot meal and
    wishes a bit of liquid refreshment and so it
    washes its mouth on the shore and drinks the sea
The sea is impassive and keeps waving as it is
    being consumed as though it didn't care or didn't
    know that it might never again be seen by me
And now the cloud has completely consumed the sea
There is no Sun
There is no sea
And the dirty gray cloud is satisfied and it picks
    its teeth on various telephone poles as it works
    its way up the hill toward my house

DAN CULLETON

TO WM. BLAKE IN HELL

Over the cold waters, president and peon pass,
one way and one way only, cross into darkness;
Charon's bark bobs always empty on recircuit;
for mortals there is no return from hell.

While kings prepare their wise orations,
a Helen now for whom none may plan,
whose loins excite the fates of nations
loiters restlessly along the strand.

On that dark morning, steel doors
clanged shrilly; it is said
Bonhoeffer smiled:
so fierce the divinty visited on man.

We do not live our lives out week by week,
nor dead long lie within our graves;
the surf froths white and seahawks shriek,
for Cuchulain wrestles with the waves.

The poets have sung
the madness which is flesh;
across the dark waters, Avilion
dissolves in phosphorescent mists.

The momentousness in our hearts
and the triviality of our lives
spin in a blinding dance
the circles of heaven and hell.

29

He who set the torch to Troy
and watched the topless towers burn
brought his son home a plundered toy
and embraced his wife with true concern.

The gates of hell are the gates of life;
we are crucified upon
the savage mandala of twisted nerves
that blossoms on the bone.

RAYMOND DALLOLIO

All you people
you think you're smart
You prey in steeples
with blackest hearts.
In that shrine,
where god is gold
you count each and every
penny you stole.
Money is worth
what money buys
but money ain't worth
perpetual lies.
Your arian race
is silver and gold
Your soul will die young
and you will die old.
You play that game
in pace with time
always the same,
always the line.
Why can't you win?
Can't you tell?
Earth's heaven
is heaven's hell.

BETSY DAVIS

PREDICATE JOHNSON

You sit
        as if the world is chair,
You smile
        at agony's statistics.

30

You watch
      as troops take over towns,
You see
      that they should seem to win.

You dine
      as if you'd earned the food,
You sleep
      when you have said your prayers.

You speak, dear sir,
      but who will listen . . . now?

LANDSCAPE

The river wanders to the sea
      tree by tree, complacently,
and leaping out to gather in
      a wave does spin a tale for fishermen,
who watch the ocean pensively
      as it saunters to its shores,
trailing in its slimey hand
      a piece of planet made of sand,
upon whose edges weep unhappy crabs
      and dead things from the deep,
while overhead a patch of sky
      enables still-life geese to fly
their yearly journey to the south —
      yet underneath their tireless wings
you'll catch Man disrupting things . . .

DELIVERANCE

Look into the future, tell me what you see — ?
      "I see a giant octopus, beneath a mushroom tree . . .
      This octopus eats kids like me, grows one yard per day,
      While all around without a sound the people try to say:
      'All we want is bread and love, no matter what the way' . . . "
About this octopus, I say, what are we to do — ?
      "We're to use our heads, I guess, and think it up a zoo??"
Now, what if no zoo holds the beast — our minds can go so far —
      "Then we must stick together, as we rush from bar to bar."

31

FROM INSIDE A SHIRT

a life is a wool shirt in winter, a shell for a self /
which shirt self wears / it's all the same whether loom /
or womb / thinks up the weave and the colors / however
whatever is in comes out in the Wash / in spite of type dye
or smart seamstress /

a life is an arm's length away from its resources /
a watcher of washers from the inside / and yet so much
more / ! / shirt styles should vary with surface essentials
of self / : / the unchaffing collar / the well-fitted sleeve /
shall all return to cocoon of infinity /
      — forever foodstuff for moths —
in dead dreaded shreds /

a life is a searching wool shirt in winter / in endless
pursuit of the right pair of slacks / yet there is the
thing / like when two single selves make some scene / they
just burst at their seams / then go for a patch / and
variations on that glad seam /
      lone shells for selves are
not perfect, immutable /

a modified lamb is a wool shirt in winter / a potential
shell for shirts for our selves / a lamb is not man, but it
could be / the biggest itch suffice it to say / is a sweat-
shirt on sundays /
      Let Us Scratch / . . . /

do not shrug self at shoulders of life / nor shell soiled
selves off by the ream / remember that all selves can
burst at the seams / even the wildest wooliest shirt
wrinkles / slowly with wear and with scratching and
shrugging /
      a hole might appear /

and *OH* the panic of nudeness / the horror of needing needles /
/ ! / the holy wool shirt in winter is death for the self / for
out through the hole and onto the snow / dribbles self when
      the Holy Last Wearing arrives / . . . /

by now you have guessed that what i express / can be crammed
into one little nutshell:
      A fool is a self such as I that is thinking it's secure
and toughshit when inside its shirt shell.

WHITE MAN'S BURDEN

Bomb the Cong. Starve them out.
Freedom wins. Please don't shout.
in your dorm. Stay in line. please.
don't conform. Love your neighbor.
if he's poor. Hate political
affairs. like ignore bores.
    and listen here.
    do. this. all.
    simultaneously.

H. L. DE WYS

YOU AND I

Born out of full nearness
Searching embracing arms
hands that ordain
Stimulates
What might give
Or is grounded
Passive chained
Signed away
In selfcontending refrain
You and I
Whose rhythm
Rimes intertwining approaches
Guided guiled
In conscious poses
Of I caress
Sweet lips
Lisping silent questions
The sharing bearing
Of each pulses
The drumbeat
Of tight skinned motions
Envelope other
Closer, closer
Closer, closer
Closer, closer
Approaching one
In full concentric vibrations
Bubbling out of eternal spring
Whose tension elates
Dilates and ebbs away
What is left
We care in tenderness
You and I

33

OLÉ

The stage
Encased darkness
Light erased spaces
Wood lined floor
In center
The dancer
High up
Brows curved
Contemplates
The stringing, singing tones
Of fingered strings
The guitar hugged
By accompanying creator
Upon the bare chair
In his introspective pose
The heels
With their tight staccato potential
Rap the first strove
Of from top arrived motions
Whose impulses
Curve along the slender lines
Of the tensed up body
The arms balance it all
The floor resounds
The rhythmical dimensions
Of passionate cadence
Stops by finishing ruffle
The inner spaced silence
Gives birth to more tender touch
Then again the passionate strokes
Full and flowing
Going, going
But always controlled
Mastered, behold the song
Reveals and sings with the strings
Of loving
Folkways
Historic bonds
Spontaneous joys
And gay abandon
The everlasting gypsy song

BIG BROTHER 1967

The loudspeaker
Full of voices
Which are noises
Talking over
Idioms not experienced
Facts not understood
Distorted observations
Throb into my ear
Disturb my mind
By their unkindness
To be screened out
And disappear

ALEXANDER N. DMITRIEV

THREE POEMS

Four and one half tears fell
No more, no less.
That's all that could be spared
For that individual.
Everyone was saving up for another day.
A day when they would cry for themselves.

He was a good person,
His intentions as a whole were noble.
He could not help being ignorant at times,
He was young yet,
And even elders can be fools.

Maybe it was for the best
That he died.
Everyone said it was.

Cast upon a moonlit sea
Sailing for the Acropolis,
My heart dying after every beat.
I must return to where I was born
To find my remains among the ancient bones
And there place my bleeding heart.

Old papers fly down the street
Passing everyone and everything with their speed.
But motion is relative,
Look close — it is not the papers flying forward
It is us going backward.

A. H. DRUMMOND

In
the dance,
the sweating bodies,
the hands slapping
the floor —
squeeking —
the hard-breathing
guts
with grace evoke
all our
now and future past.

STEPPING OUT

I climb out of the subway
behind a lady
with a newly bandaged thumb
into
the high windowed cliffs
and slices of sunlight.
On the sidewalk
I pass the lady
and walk quickly
to the light
at the end of the block.

When I walk across a new cornfield,
it is hard to step from ridge to ridge.
The spacing isn't right.
My gait is larger than the furrows will allow.
But then,
leaping one is awkward too.

GOD

Cast adrift
on
cement shores,
we lay gasping,

BLESS

gasping;
our gills atrophy
and we air-breathe
frantically,
learning.

NEW YORK

Waves pound pilings
and rip-rapped rocks
in eternal collision.
We, the children
of innocence
(murmuring refugees —
culture shocked/
starved),
are beckoned
by Sirens
who bestow on us
a violent grace
as we press
against
their intricate anatomy.

PAMELA EDE

GUILTY MEADOWS

Electra mornings mourning
dark dimmer dreams
never dreamed
dripping with succulent scent
as I approach him with reproach
begging electra kisses dripping
sweet sour sauce
committing the uncommitable sin
sent away
    sad

37

APOSTLES OF AUTHORITY

have Compassion for that policeman
would You like to
                    breathe his air
                    carry his weapon
                    sell your soul
                                to a costume
wear Authority
                    becomes god
and all things are Done
                    in his name
and he can do nothing   Wrong
omni
                    potent
                    scient
                    present
                              Hail
have Compassion the policeman
                    walks in Fear
a c o n t i n u o u s Riot raging in
                              his own s $_o^l$ u
but he doesn't even Know it
                    and never Will

                    until?

MOUNT OLYMPUS

Cold, empty in all its barrenness
Where have all the people gone?
A long time in changing
Where have all the real gods gone?
They were married when man
began changing whose hearts
were stirred to new fulfillment
The mold of the old no longer fitting
Leaving the flower a mere seed
the sparkle a half lit glow
Liberty reduced to bonds
Where has the chorus gone?
Out to compose cantatas comple-
menting the vogue of their voices

Where have all the confused
souls gone? Out
To transform their god, everything
A temple with no altar
              no steeple
The only dogma being
              I love you

RICK ELDRIDGE

FIRST CUTTING

It was the time of day,
he told me later,
that he was sure
that bale fell
(seeming to slowly heave itself
off the load)
with express intent
to break his back.
(And it nearly did, too,
but that he felt it coming
and stepped instead of stopped.)

Still, someone had to shake him hard
to wake that sundown time of day;
and when next cutting came around,
he preferred to work
  on top the load.

WHEAT FIRE

It had gotten away from us —
then turned on its own wind
and drove us back —
thirty shovelpiked strawknights
sprintscattering back to bunch and watch
the dragon throat tonguelash
the clouded dark with sparks
until it burst —
and rolled and thundered
down a morning
of grey sheets on us
and him — the one
that lost by fire,
and now by dawn and rain.
—Maybe we can still save some —
he said.

THE FRESHMAN: THE TURNING POINT

The door was open —
and he,
the young brown man,
offered beer
though we had never spoken,
then spoke through empty space
too quickly to delay the need
for words.

I being young as well,
offered tobacco,
and found soon enough
my book and pen in mute sleep
as the first numb disbelief
of waking unquiet
searched the lamplight
in steady words —

Steady —
but for a flickering tremor
that passed, time and time,
like a blind wraith
among the canted lights and shadows
of the old house.

The mind has its ghosts as well,
but with him there lay the dead,
still warm —
as he spoke, I dreamt,
and felt a stir
in the smiling but unquiet sleep
that lulls old wounds.

He asked me:
— what is all this for?
and much later, when I said
— for good,
not knowing what truth would prove;
he thanked me for my time, and left.

I listened to his footsteps
down the mawed black
of the stairwell,
drifting up
like carpeted heartbeats
of old lives.

EARLY MADNESS

A spring night
in the ghost face
of
January:

I lie on my back
in the dustdry haysmelling
grass
watching the tattered sky,
the blue grey stormwater of
heavens
shifting
among the first scouting stars.

The dark breath
of time alien
spring
moves upon my soulnakedness.

My lover kisses
my being
with lips new-drunk
with the water of summer thunder
and I become her limbs
of fire
and taste the earthsalt
of her breast in my mouth —
and we
become
each other,
in the ecstacy,

the feversweet afterrain
of pagan grass —
where stars become
fireflies burning on the blades
that close above,
the curtain canopy
of our bed
of madness.

A spring night in January.
A new rose
on the face
of the snow.

JUNE 26

There is a small breeze
that wanders in and out
like a wistful little girl
in a dress of night.

The highway has stopped whining
and is cooled and fitful
passing of fast and late
or eyes of early routes.

The aimless breeze hums with
hard lights at the scale
and at the dumps where
dusty eyes wait for rain

which starts the growing grey
east with flat puffs of
powder dust, then runs the
black passing slick with dawn.

JOHN L. ERLICH

UPSIDE DOWN CHILD

Taster of all the world,
How does it feel
To know something new
In every grasp of a slight hand?

However I may turn you,
You smile
And put your fingers in your mouth.
How does it feel?

There is no distance through which
You will not try to reach.
How does it feel
To be the universe?

How does it feel
To be tied in diapers,
Fed by monsters,
To play with things that are not you?

MARY EVERETT

The here
We fear
And wait
For it
To pass.
Once gone
We long
For it
To be
Once more.

SOMEBODY DIED

Somebody died when the tide came in
When the moon slid behind the clouds
When old Cid's wife threw the dishwater out
When the sea was suddenly still.

"Somebody died," the fishmonger cried
When he saw the boots float to the shore.
"It must have been Andrew Yates,"
Said the drunkard at Alex's Bar.

"I knew him. Was long ago."
"Killed himself." The rumors spread.
"Speared with a harpoon. Jumped into the sea.
Quarreled with young Molly Brown."

"Andrew Yates, who was he?" a traveler said.
"Jumped into the sea when the tide came in,"
The village explained of the dead
Whose boots was all they had seen.

Come the breeze
To shake your leaves,
Poplar trees,
To show all these
Other trees
Your bright silver coins.

PETER FARLEKAS

It was so easy
to take you away.
I loosed your hand
when I stooped
cutting a daffodil.
Then the storm began
and you were gone.

WAIT

Singers, singing their songs,
minstrels with their tambourines,
sun-lit days of meadow larks,
this is like our lives now.
Waiting for our lives to begin,
to sing our songs together,
to light our candle to the world.
This is the spring of our reawakening.
And pin wheels flying
in carnival-splendor ablaze
with the stars spelling your name tonight
this is how I love you.
Holding on to you
through all our tears and laughter,
through all the years we will have together,
this is how it will be.
Till that day, till that time,
I will spend spinned-out time
whispering your name to four walls
as I wait for you.

In a time not too unlike these times —
a time of sun-lit memories and vagrant breezes
old maids and misers
raised up their shades into the full glory
of their bloomed out of door chrysanthemums.
Trellised walks all too quickly
held and spilled two by too many clasped lovers.

Lovers cradling their hearts in their throats
spewed them forth constantly in words
caught up in the nets of their beloved's eyes.
And one day I came stumbling and all too blind
and alone into your world and into your life.
Gradually I began to see and the people
who surrounded us became
crystalline figurines which only
reflected you.
The streets you walked were piecemealed
fashions of topsy-turvy fabricated material
and I followed you through them
adoring you and everything of you.
If there had been times of unwarranted indecision
before, they were gone then
for you received all I had to give
like a dreamer dreaming and draining a full cup
before a flowered mirror.
Tonight the wind drives the rain across
my window sill.
Trying tormented to gain entrance into my room,
those stopped fall dying and dead
like wearied warriors held in one another's arms.
Your footsteps on the stairs at last.
A moment later I know you stand behind me
and reaching out my hand I hold yours
a little tighter for all the time gone from me.
"I love you, you know."
And looking back I am struck by your
god awful beauty just as the
very first time we met.
Quietly and swiftly I am in your arms.
Later, much later, when the rain
has ended and there is a soft wind
from out of the south, I hear you say
in the darkened room,
"I dreamed a long time ago
that I would like a red balloon
more than anything else in the world."
And the oleandered wallpaper
is the last thing we see as sleep slips
like a warm glove
around, through, and into us.

It is a paradox.
Mothers crying for those dead
while those becoming mothers
weep for their new life.
Those war dead and dying,
limbs shoveled into garbage cans
as cripples beg of the sightless.
Life.
We never made it our time,
it was always a hand-me-down.
We knew it.
Yet our anger erupted bar-room brawls
while nations made bombs
like candles fierce.
We weren't in too bad a year
when we died.
And now bastards crawl
from nativity's rot,
their umbilical cords
hanging from their mouths
to stand upright
to this
the new man.

THOMAS FERENCE

ALL NIGHT

All night I hear the streetcars
All night I feel the flash of neon

And dreary in the morning I see
The church-going multitude but

I have no church and I step
Downstairs to an Italian bar.

All night Sunday I sip quietly
All night Sunday I slip slowly

Monday dawns freely, showering
Me over with rampant radiance,

But it's cold outside and I step
Downstairs to an Italian bar.

The snow swirls and eddies in
The streets outside but I

Have no place to go and all
Night Monday I sip in silence.

Tuesday dawns majestically and I stir
Early in my skin, throw a blanket

Round my shoulders and begin to write.
The words come hard at first for there's

A taste in my mouth but soon it leaves
And the images roll from my fingertips.

All day Tuesday I sit and write and
At last I have three soiled pages,

Three soiled pages, poems to the world
And misty I look out and wish thru the cold

Life were now but time leads on
And my hands push forward.

About nine o'clock it begins to snow
And as I read the lines once again I

Begin to see much of myself and my
Life emerge from the sweat-stained cuplets.

Tears flow as again I see myself alone
And all night I hear the streetcars

All night I feel the flash of neon
And all night I cry.

MICHAEL FIDLER

KISS

Kiss — let mine be more than bliss
let mine bring you down, compel you
overwhelm you, ecstatic emphatic
let it throw off every strip
let it spread your toes and fingertips
and of course your thighs.
let me hear whimpers and cries
feel nails tearing my flesh
and impatient breath, beckoning
let it burst your mind
and the overripened find
that I search, seek — beseech.
no command, expand its grand
shrill scream — break!

47

TO WHERE?

Restrained by resignation to one position
held helpless by a demanding society
freedom is financial, frustration festers
seeking solution by schooling, delaying
a dependent student, years of decaying

Escape; the essential of existence
from what? to where? to anywhere?
in mind? in body? totally?
We suck deeply and taste sweetly
for moments, which may master us

ALONE IN A CLASSROOM

Rows of mirror surfaced seats in military silence.
Facing forward, watching black rectangles clouded by chalk.
Scribblings from minds; some stir memories, others make no sense.
Windowless walls once were bombarded with Incessant talk.
Softly colored, humbly, they are resting, waiting for more.
They have heard much, though not reflecting upon its value.
The loud humming of machines can be heard through the door,
With its even smoothness of silent noise beckoning you
To become part of the still, unhurried tranquility.

Your mind is dimmed in the content of faint thought.

The thin ice of stillness slides you slowly, gently.
No more stiff chairs or dirty black squares.
Gone are the four walls, the universe, the burdening body.

Tap! Crack!
The ice is shattering, voices are clattering.
It's footsteps in the forgotten halls.
The chairs are again relaxed to fit the human form.
Once again the walls reflect the baffling, babbling sound.
Peacefulness gone, back again is the human storm,
The four walls, the universe, the body — the mind is bound.

J. D. FINK

SIX POEMS

I saw a man floating in a boat,
    changing his clothes.
On with one suit, slip out of another,
    freely he chose,
To throw each suit in its turn
    out of the boat.
And put on another.
Monkcy in the middle
    to a sun that flies
    from side to side
    in his sky.

    you know when you wake up in the m
  orning sometimes things just look so b
  eautiful and happy. you cant help but thi
  nk happy thoughts — about trees and sun an
  d even little kids when theyre not being brats
or need their diapers changed. even though you
know some people who could use their minds ch
anged it doe   snt really both   er you cu
z youll love   them anyway.   you think
of dew drop   s and roses'   thorns t
hat prick bu   t dont really   hurt cuz
the petals ar   e so   soft   . the sme
ll of moss in the fores   t and the tingle of
warmth as you step o   ut of the shade ma
kes you so happy to   be alive today an
d why cant this go   on forever. it sh
ould — all good things should be forever. you lov
e life so much and the people in it that you just
never want to leave them, any of them. people
  mean so much to you — theyre your whole l
  ife no no no no no no no no no no pleas
  e help no no no no no no no no no let m
  e stay no no no no no no no no no a li
  ttle? no no no no no no no no no why
  why? no no no no no no no no no no im
  sad no no no no no no no no no i
    dont really fear death
    i hate leaving friends

Wine-witches wander scattering
                              flowers
while seven men sit and plot a
                              war.
Godmen sit and mend their gods
                    to
fit the men who figure the odds
                         that there is a God.
            March winds blow a herald
            to Spring and flowers who
            grow on the graves of the
            slow,   while
            the fast linger on with weeds in their mouth.
The house of mud stands
in sparkling glory
and the dirt-hens
scratch for seed.
Home burns as water hardens in the veins of men in vain,
as women sit and lay on command, like dogs in an act.
You choose your wife from a three ring circus
and housebreak her to love.

I'm drowsy today.
I can't write or move my pen
   to free myself
   from the ground where I grow
   more impatient to sleep my thoughts
                    and keep my thoughts
   for my own sugar,
                 and not loan a cup
            to keep my neighbor.

For my use,
I'd sugar cakes and pastries,
   and delicate confections, and
   trade them to children for sugary smile.

But my neighbor betrays the sweet to her own end
                 at the beginning of her day,
                    to dispel the night
                 that lingers in her eye;

Sugar
in a cup of bitter.
For my neighbor must see and hear in tones
                    that are clear — and not
be drowsy.

50

you take your love and hand
it out like free samples
of a salesman selling
himself. stay to yourself.
don't whore your mind to the
blind clowns that pack
into cars that circle the
circus ring. they go nowhere and all
fit in because nothing
is in them. empty clown suits
with cash register smiles
that take their toll as you're
pushed through the aisle
by the white-caned
crowd.
pick yourself and shovel your
grave, make your body in plaster
as you like it, and bury it. and
show your friends where you lie.
the show must go on.

take your love lightly in your
pocket and walk your eyes in their
sockets — till you see another
sneaking from their grave
to live.

Windows and sunglasses, clowns smile and novocaine words
are brick and stone that build the world's walls
and give man prisons for his enemies, and himself
a place to hide.
Each man alone walks his own corridor, long silent steps
through death row while lights dim
as a quiver of power replaces the humanity that dwelled
in the next cell.
But then occasionally
occasionally there's a crack in the wall
a crack — and a nervous smile
a startled look from darting eyes,
and both run on.
— and return, to search for the crack
and to widen it.

MICHAEL PETER FINNEY

DISAPPOINTMENT

Alone in a twentieth century,
With god and world peace as dead ideals,
   but existing;
And love and truth in compromise and settlement;
A desperate grasp on one's life nonetheless.

Self lost in individual-collective confusion,
In being what your neighbors are,
And being what they should be;
Loving your neighbor as yourself.

Creativity lost in analysis and criticism,
Spirit drowned in a clatter of placards,
Hair hiding more than a human face;
Inward youth of an outward world.

With roots in the past and seeds in the stars
A birth is sought to be aborted,
A promise made short.

HERE I

Grow up again? different circumstances? new personality?
   why? difference? Sure. can't help it, could be worse.
     sure could!
What to do with now, dream, pass each day like today,
   then what? another scotch, another beer,
     Truth is what is.
       Hope is what could be,
        Future is what was before it was,
       so no hope except, maybe.

THERESA B. FOLAN

A CYNIC SPEAKS

Ah, deceit, you wear
So many masks.
Yesterday, a smile.
Today, a touch.
Tomorrow, what?
Sincerity, oh, yes.
Or, perhaps truth,

Or, prayerful hands.
A guise of innocence
So carefully planned.
The defeated look
Of the martyr.
So sorry for failing.
Ah, yes, so sorry.
But, all the while
Seeking tender spots
Of broken hearts.
Then too, there's love.
Ah, yes, well done.
A certain winner
With the lonely.
And, oh, yes, belief.
Here, a brilliant conqueror
Even with the non-lonely.
And peacefulness too.
It has such power
Over the unsuspecting.
And, what about God,
The Master Trickster?
In the warm sunshine,
Or, in frightening thunder,
There too, your presence.

Ah, deceit, you wear
So many masks.

PETER FORD

THOUGHTS ON THE EMERGENCE TO CONSCIOUSNESS
OF INANIMATE OBJECTS

(when i am alone) a 40-armed 80-legged night with 10 groins
rapes my brain: its crackcrazy sidewalks grabkick twistlunge
windowmad its buildings as dogmouthed roads dayraged foam tar
i sprint for home
and chair

but now a two-armed four-legged chair with one throat
sings me a song (and now i'm not alone): frankly i'd
rather go sleep on the lawn!

FIVE POEMS

god's name's whichwhat
since his any's made of thisthat
if his every's full of purest
so's his each god how obscene

—how obscene do i mean?
!purely obscene —

like an unused excuse me condom
or an old twot i beg your pardon

god whose name's whatwhich
has an every made of thatthis
since his any's full of maddest
his each's my how sane

—how sane's sane?
!maddingly sane —

like a whore in love
like duck-crud

god whose name's thatthis
has an any made of whatwhich
if his every's full of sorriest
his each's your how glad

—how glad's glad?
!sorry, i can't say —

maybe gladder than you'll understand
god knows

for god's name's obscenest
since his any's made of pure
if his every's full of sanest
so's his each our how mad

—how mad do i mean?

!!!gladly madly if sanely obscenely since sorrily purely
my-your-ourly
who're in love

poem has a pretty whole
(reminds me of a mind taking heart)

poem has a pretty that is a pretty hard whole to make i mean
(reminds me of a heart leaving flesh)

(but hellbent that god knows i am
between these heavens of my mind)
i take her o so littlest soul

(& leaving big my heart's leg on her littler flesh)
i make her o so little whole

try standing on your head
in your own excretion
in a dark hot room
that's not much bigger than you

& the floor gives way
& you drop head-first down a chute
& some bastard grabs you
& he knocks the breath into you

& you'll know how it feels to be born

dead is made of not to make
and not to make is made of hate:
hates jampacked with minus a moon,
chockfull of starless hates without sun
(or even a flashlight)
hates brimfilled with minus a sky,
flushstocked with earthless hates without sea
(or even a puddle)
hates glutstacked with minus a soul,
cramstuffed with heartless hates without whole
(or even a titty)

so down with dead and up with love:
let's make-to-have-to-be and live!

life love & the pursuit
(rooti-toot toot toot):

o men are for bedding
& women for wedding

life love & the pursuit
(rooti-toot toot toot):

if girls are for marrying
when boys are for tarrying
(when men are for maling
if women are railing),
then wives are for cheating
& husbands for beating

life love & the pursuit
(rooti-toot toot toot)

ROBERT FRANKLIN

LILITH

O beautiful tender child!
   My flaxen haired fairy;
Followed have I
   Tho the way was wild.
Tis as if in a dream
   We've lain beside
The streams.
   Whilst ecstasy deformed
The sense of time
   And my life was consumed
By a love divine.
   Each spring a lance
Seems to impale my heart
   At the sight of the first
Rose in bloom;
   For together we decreed
The Dark Gospel to be hallowed;
   By the Prism, the Flute,
And the Loom.

THE QUEST

My name? Ah but void am
    I of name.

Absurb you say? Precisely why
    I came.

Probed have I?
    To the doors of the ill-famed,
Where the ultimate in ecstasy
    Is obtained:

Through the sheperd's lea;
    To the mystic floors of the sea,

Over the mountains, shoeless
    And lame,

Through the monasteries of the
    Eminently ordained;

Searched have I through the
    Crematory dross of the predestined
Claimed,

Into the abyss of the insane,
    To the profound hell devoid
Of flame.

Ah! but alas! My quest has been
    Futile and in vain,

Tis avowed that my psyche shall
    Never roam nor reign.

Scrutinize your log-books o keeper
    Of the names;

Search them well for my name!
    For I am the —
"Grandfather of *CAIN!*"

FORGOTTEN — BUT NOT GONE

My body shall find not itself in
       Darkness
Among black thoughts of severer
       Harshness
Than that of a cold headstone.
       Not one of all the mortal world
Shall rest
       His fleshy head upon my bony,
gnarled chest.
       But no more tears — save the
Salty dew that wets my grassy bed;
       Shall ever show my dark unfathomed
Pride — nor an epitaph quote the life
       That I have bled.

KAREN AILEEN FRIEDMAN

ONCOMING STORM

Of a sudden, sunlight dips behind a pregnant
Cloud. And as the cloud gives birth to several others,
The formerly yellowed sky turns to grey
For lack of light. And the sun itself, imprisoned
Behind the grey clouds, makes a final effort
To save the scurrying people below
With a sudden flash of light. But, defeated by
The new-born cloud, the sun is once
Again imprisoned. And tiny drops of rain fall
With increasing speed toward the ground.

NANCY GALL

METAMORPHOSIS

I find it delicious,
This feminine world I was justnow born in-to.
Justnow a delicious knowledge and realization
Of me
Signed my second birth certificate
And said "Hello" in a soft and gentle voice.
Sinking into a pillow world at night
I am a woman
In my dreams and, oddly enough, in my un-dreams.
When I awake,
I stretch long and hard.
I am womanbeginning.

ON BECOMING DEAD

Listen: to my mind,
Listen: to my heart.
They are going mad,
Wrapped in swaddling clothes and lying in a gutter,
Crying and feeling sorry for themselves,
Knowing what they did created a full crux of fixation,
Knowing that they have seen and not believed and
That life is hell and Man is dead and God never lived.
We two — the mind and heart — are dead.
We wonder if we will be resurrected. (We doubt it.)
So far, the white nun has not harassed us. (We wish
        someone would.)
They lied to us in church. "Death be not proud."
We died and waited but God did not come to weigh our
        rights and wrongs. ("All my good deeds wasted!")
We are waiting, waiting, waiting. Will anything happen?
Must we sit here and be eternally bored
Because of a slip of the foot like the father
        of Don Juan's lover?
We are dead, and we can do nothing by ourselves.

SO I CAN DIE

All the things I tried to do were never done.
I forced all the people I loved to turn away.
I scraped rotting filth from stinking gutters
In dank alleys.
I threw the filth on all the works of art in the world.
I cheerfully magnified ugliness. I horrified lovely people.
I picked up crystal glasses and threw them down, and I was
Screaming in delight.
I took rocks and smashed in the soft heads of newborns.
I ripped baptismal curtains and cursed at rabbis.
I mocked the minds of the Great and
Added lines to new maps to confuse people.
I cried and no one had touched me.
I screamed for I was a woman and I hated the woman I was.
Yes, I could see I was slipping into, slipping into
Hells, slightly below the surface of earth and
I could see nothing but black, Black, *BLACK*.
Oh, world, leave me alone,
So I can die quietly.

I PLAYED ALIVE

I came home today.
You were dead.
You were dead and once upon a time,
You lay in bed with a woman you loved
And made me.
I came home today, and I hugged fat people.
You were dead.
It was my fault. I had gone away and left you alone.
I came home and everyone tried to hug me.
(Finally, I could help you; it's easy to help the dead.)
I came home today and you were dead.
You were dead and my life-soul went to heaven with you.
Oh, oh, you were dead.

SUMMERTIME

Shadows scratching the ground as the sun scoots distractedly
        around the earth . . .

Still child, seated C-shaped, legs spread,
        a boy's vision sucking into Memory
        every movement of a knobbily-built ant . . .

Hot pavement, bare feet.

Dirty, sticky sand ingrained in the fingernails of a
        I-wish-I-were-naked lad,
        His sandbox an unlocked door to China . . .

Dirty bra and slip strap-handles decorating
        warm, tanned shoulders . . .

Dirtiness and grittiness.

Hands perfumed as their sweat mingles with osmotic lemonade
        in cheap free-from-the-milk-man glasses . . .

Laziness, listlessness.

60

INSIDE INFORMATION

I speak from the inner etiology,
And I am a woman of truth and courage.
I make babies during the commercials;
I hear the cry of a thousand paid political ads.
I wish for slim editions of the Bible in Greek.
Tall high chairs fill the kitchen in my house,
And I have no aspirin in the medicine chest — only LSD.
I walk behind blue eye shadow and
I see the world between stripes of Very Black mascara.
So what if I wear no slip?
So what if my children go hungry?
Follow me, and I will make you fish-men.

PATRICIA TONI GALLANT

EN PASSANT

Oh, burning, burning, thou hast come,
To beat upon this fervent drum.
To see this magic of the heart,
And deep within to cast thy dart;
Thou curséd pain I feel so deep,
Has now succumbed to quiet sleep.

THE QUEST

The wind blew like a fervent breath,
And spoke soft words to me.
The world about was like a fire,
And opened its flames to see.

I walked into its waiting arms,
With love my every thought.
His meaning was my path in life,
And all that I had sought.

But then the flame came closer,
And wrapped me in its pleat.
It burned my heart too quickly,
With no warning, only heat.

It scared me out of loving,
And set my heart all free.
And then the fire vanished,
And with it, it freed me.

61

EXISTENCE

The lacy substance of clouds to come,
The beating of the midnight drum.
Existence to its full extent,
The overwhelming trees, unbent.
The mirrors of a life to see,
The sparkling joys of ecstasy.
Silver rings around the moon,
And the softness of a favorite tune.
The shining rainbow, after wet,
Forming a silk-like, filmy net.
But when to touch it, you will find
It evaporates into sublime.
What is it all, the real, the not,
The rainbow's end, with Golden Pot?
What is the meaning, could it be
A simple, pretty fantasy?

THE DRAGON

The big brave man came walking by,
And the little men all gave a sigh.
The big brave man walked to the Dragon,
While the little men watched with nary a rag on.
The big brave man let out a roar,
And then was killed by the Dragon's paw.

THERE IS GOOD, IN THE WORST OF US

Such a big man looks small,
When someone wiser and bigger comes along.
Such a mean man looks kind,
When rigor mortis sets in.
Such a brave man looks frightened,
When he knows he can do no more.
Such a phony one hates,
Is no longer hated after defeat.
And someone insincere is smirked at,
Until someone has been insincere to him.

SALTED WINGS

My love came flying by — like a bird at its fullest speed.
I reached up to grab it — but it fell at my grasp.
I clung to its salted wings — and sang love to it.
Then the salt was too much weight for it,
And my love died.

JAMES G. GARDNER

the child had yet to celebrate its first birthday
ash blond hair and short forehead, silver eyes, three front teeth
    in a minute mouth on a slender face
head seeping through a thick neck to a thicker body
the first fruit of newly marrieds, screaching tears in the unknown night
mothered with lotioned hands, calmed by the subtoned voice
of a proud father hardly ventured from the mother's warmth
to the father's eyes enfolded,
when pronounced by the doctors: sick
malformed in the lower intestines
duodenum fused to liver
muscle spasms and lack of breath
pronounced by the doctors on the backporch of its infancy: sick
preoperative probings: dabbing, slitting, layer by layer abdomen
    rolled back, prodding the intestines: stomach, liver, lungs
retreat, reclosing, then the final stitching
closing shut the erratic patchwork of contused and lost organs
the doctor's final verdict: sick, without hope

with the parent's consent to storm the walls of hopelessness
the surgeons today will reenter the child
white masks covering the mouths that spoke: hopeless
and the same hands that probed the child's inner wasteland are newly
sterilized today — in fact within the next hour — the scapel will
    try again in a shadowed operating theater
while i'm sitting in a washington park, receiving a suntan, trying to
    write a poem to ask: why so young?
freak miscarriages of nature such as this should happen only
to the old, already expected to die, long beyond their usefulness
but once a person is loved that love cannot be shut off like the blood
    in a pinched artery
and the aged have a lifetime of love cultivation behind them
it should happen only to five month old babies
loved by no one but the mother and father
this, i would think, is justification enough for life
it shouldn't happen to anyone, old or young
yet death is indiscriminate in its stalking
and we all run in fear of our livers failing, or our lungs deflating,
    or our hearts freezing
writing a poem in the open air and sun will not change this,
will not alter the distance of our running or the speed
it will not even transform the outcome of today's operation
if the child dies on the table, plunged with a healing blade,
so do we all — if it survives, we are all given another chance
to find a better hiding place.
how futile!

the voices of the multitudes of mankind murmur in my mind
soliloquies and monologues, odes to brown sunken fern trees
all grotesquely funny, all grotesquely real
proportionless images of inner designs
all obviously meaningless, yet touched by the reticent reach of reality
i even sometimes expect god to hook into the hotline to my sub-conscious
and enlighten me as to whom or what i should save
what masses of humanity i should lead out of suppression into glory
or what lake or river or stream or sewer leak i should part
for easy passage and how much toll i should charge
i see the army of humiliation marching into battle
i hear the clump-clump-clump of thick soled boots
i see the field strewn with blood gory corpses
goliath the philistine slain by little david with anemic sling
i see a young man with a bullet smashed forehead
lying under sheltering asian palms
i can hear his groans of agony, his crys, death slaughtered dreams,
bloodpool eyes, soldier of the king, david with death machine trampled
      by the goliath of inescapable commitment
yet oozing from the oriental landscape, from the lands back home,
      from those inexhaustable springs of mind
are voices, fighting the hawks and doves, commie, capitalist,
and know-it-all hypocrite voices everpresent, everspeaking
since the dawn of man's first rocked hostility
to the era of his atomic-powered hate:
the man, be he slant eyed or round, yellow, or black, or white, or red
coming from the right or wrong side of those infamous tracks
is a man: not a pig to be butchered, nor a tool to be toyed with,
      not an instrument of policy, nor the regrettable result of environment
but a man, enshrined in the sacred grotto of soul

o my children, for you i cry
inheritors of the rubble which we
inherited from our fathers, passing
it once again on to you, shabbier still
our fathers ventured smiling from the womb of decadence
we were born of the upsurge of world slaughter, reaching
      maturity with a single sonic holocaust
and you were begotten of that awkward doldrum which
      we called peace
yes: our historical dowry was much deficient
and we, with the opulence of blinded optimists, squandered
      that little
after this, what have we to give you

64

that we have not already prostituted?
teeth in our time have been enough gnashed
(emitting shooting sparks of mad machine gun bullets)
weeping in our time has been sufficiently done
(flooding lives with single tearful booms)
before us we had the future and its exhaustless resources
    as hope, but we
were fool enough to take it and play with it as if it were
    some sort of toy
so that we have to leave to you as inheritance nothing
but a loathsome past, surging in haunting phantoms
to frustrate whatever you might attempt with the future
but you have discovered something which we had, but never
realized you have yourselves as hope, a potential far
    greater than anything we tried to manufacture
o my children, tread through the crystal city
with padded feet and velvet cloaks

three years ago
in the damp and soggy rainforest of discovery
my spirit died, and my body became a zombie
macaws cawed in the jungle trees
and deadly vipers in the twining roots hissed
as the booted feet of other explorers
stomped through the undergrowth
in search of wisdom
the thudding of the machete
battling with the hanging tubers of vines
resounded in the oppressive air
and disturbed the macaws in their cawing
and the vipers in their hissing
strike strike strike and down falls an impending tree
that in its falling reveals my spirit
prone dead on the spanish moss
three years ago
my body was an empty grave
in search of a suitable corpse
            the wind chanted in my ears
                empty   empty
my body was a gothic castle
lacking an armored governor
            the wind chanted in my ears
                empty   empty

65

my body was a deserted fun house
where passing identities frolicked in the reflections
            the wind chanted in my ears
                empty   empty
my body was a multi-limbed maze
and the wind kept bumping into itself saying:
                empty   empty
before it was eaten up by a faceless minotaur
three years ago
my body turned to wax and melted
and now my animated spirit remains
running through the streets of the world
whispering into open windows saying:
                empty   empty

ROANA GELLER

ODE TO ST. PATRICK'S CATHEDRAL

The creative hand of the
artist of the skies
is forming a castle
of water and sand,
dripping the muddy
mixture downward
into rising
layers of towers,
set apart
as growing protrusions
from the rest of the
sand-coloured mass.
And the uneven towers
in unison rise —
crystallizing
to sandy grey
as the water departs —
till the last fallen drops
attach themselves
as swirling peaks
to the pinacles reaching
ever upward toward
their creator.

66

SPECTRAL SYMPHONY

The mournful cry of a cold, lonely wind pierces the shadows of
A charcoal night, and tears from the branches the lifeless leaves that
Rustle weak protests at losing their right to security. I sit alone,
Listening at my window to a symphony so weird that it shatters my hopes,
Sets fire to my faith, and my very soul is seared.
I gaze through terror-filled eyes at the ghostly halo of the moon,
And wonder how joyous life can bear to die so soon
While all the time I live — secure, yet free —
With no vision of struggle as my destiny.
But now the whining wind has blown
My courage, as the leaves, from home,
And steals my wandering mind,
Leaving my fears behind
To drift above —
Destroyer of
My love
For life.

KAREN LEE GETTIG

HUMANITY

Time — and the void
    — of confusion
    — of martyrdom
    — of hate and war
    — of intervention
Darkness — and the breadth
    — of limitlessness
    — of endless emptiness
    — of sad depravity
    — of unreality
Suspension — and the scope
    — of waiting
    — of wanting
    — of watching
    — of wandering
Necessity — and the
    — changeless unnecessaries
    — matchless needs
    —unspoken duties
. . . tokens of — *Humanity*.

67

AWARENESS

Manage the skys —
Harness your dreams —
Find rolling air, filled with the scent of birch —
Chase the cloud's shadow to the
Loftiness of the mountain —
Now — Look down —
Below you lies the shadow of reality —
Yet you are the only real, living being.

LEE A. GLADWIN

CHILD SHATTERED

From behind the ghetto window,
By aloneness violence-webbed,
    Poverty's children watch,
See us flee asphalitic day
For the night of suburbia's womb;

We glance at their window in passing,
    Smile, but never see
The flickering of each soul,
    Microcosmed there,
In a shattered pane of glass.

BAEZ AND CAST

Joan Baez beneath an armpit,
    View obscured, and
    Humanity huddled
On the earth articulate
Protests at dense-brained barriers;
Patience, "Down in front!"
    Diminishes to a
    Zealot's, "Get 'em!" —
    A couple twists
    Upon a twig
    Above nervous glances —
Baez, supported by a cast of thousands.

COMPUTERS

Blue-white tower fades
    in smog-clouded soliloquy,
Its Angelus unheard
    by each mechanicus —
Napalm blossoms flame,
    fetid smoke ascends,
Ashes reduced to digits,
Are fed to computerised men.

MONA GOLD

YOU

Midnight,
    Such a restful hour . . . for most
    But I . . . I must stay awake
    To guard your weary body
    Lying beside my equally tattered mass.

Stillness,
    Seems too still.
    Even your breath has smothered to a hush
    So one might question your mortality.
    A frightening thought . . . for most,
    But I feel the whisper of your breath upon my numbed arm
    Where your head rests.

Security, Safety,
    A feeling sought after . . . by most.

You,
    Turn or twitch.
    Some unconscious thoughts, or taunting dreams,
    You interpret by your moves,
    Keep me from sleep.

My desire to know all there is of you.
    My desperate yearning for you to awaken to my
        Loving
            Wanting and
                Needing you . . . most.

69

1966

The tomb of my brain tears to expand
    To ease the torture of the tattering tempo
    I'm forced to keep time with
        Tomorrow after tomorrow.

No let up from the outside world.
    No understanding of the fruitless campaign
    My mind conducts.

Trying to place,
    To separate the symbolic from the secure.
Symmetrical, supposedly orderly,
    But obscured from either.

Conclusively;
    conflicting atoms
        arranging themselves,
            Developing into a dilemma
                destined to destruction . . .
                    and final peace.

BRUCE LAWTON GREENE

INNOCENCE

The morning sun polished
The red woolen sleeves,
Of the blond-haired child
As she walked through the leaves,

Into worlds of color
She was quick to embark,
Silently noting
Each place she might mark,

But the dry amber leaves
Soon faded in the distance,
And revealed the harshness
Of a daily existence,

Now her platinum eyes
Await the hour,
When next she perceives,
The land of the flower.

NOCTURNAL CLEARANCE

I am walking,
The sky is clear,
The stars are out,

A leaf slowly drops to the ground,
As
    I
       Drop also,
But there are no stars in my sky.

PONDER

A cat is sleeping on a quiet night,
The earth seems far away,
Cold water flows down a naked hill,
A tree embraces the day,

A warm wind stirs the golden sand,
The moon shines on the sea,
I sit and think of newborn friends,
O where can my love be?

KAREN GRIMMER

APOCALYPSE

now,
the thought enters
to wrap like
a blanket around my
decision the reasons
for its necessity,
now to clothe in
the best-dressed silks
of rationale that
which was previously

only a need, some
swelling desire for
freedom removed from
the aching wounds of
confusion.

what was love,
desire in all its
brilliantly dark colors,
strives now to become
the more sultry
lavender of friendship
and dims briefly to
reach after the
gentler, soft seagreen
dimensions of alter-ego.

thus, in the journey
through the confident
spectrum of understanding
to break under an acceptance
(in its responsive destiny)
of my need for perpetuation
and the deeply adamant
qualities of mutual negation,
yet to acknowledge its
rightness in terms of black
lines drawn tight and forbidding
against possible deviation.

finally, in one artist's stroke
of multi-colored consciousness
to expiate from yesterday's
angered, swollen womb
of passionate discourse all
traces of violation; thus, to
portray solitary on the canvas
an awareness of scarlet life
and the knowledge that i loved
in you only some bluer latent
elements of my own potential.

MARIE YANDLE GUINN

TIRO

He stood, where many
Stood before
Courageous lad, askance
Life's riddles, present, past
Reaching far
Hands outstretched
Fingers eager to unlatch
The shrouded unrelenting catch.
Intervals of calm
but always
On the brink
The key within
A boundless reach
Moving on
inch by inch
A bursting chant
pregnating roar
A surging screaming shout
The Key, The Key
Beyond the shore
Then ebbing
On salvos of pain
Hurtling
Crushing
Blotting out
The Key. The Key
Evading source.
Surpassing reach
Transcending doubt.

WILLIAM C. HADDAN

THE NEW ROMANS

Always these brash caverns
Have the light of cherry heat
And darkness
And wooden parquet floors
Slap sandals boots and barefeet
Of girls with cotton candy hair
Or with weepy willows flying
'Round bouncing monkey shoulders.

To sit in amber nonchalance
Of sea foam mugs
And crystal cubes in glasses
With casual indifference
Caring
Staring
At the other side of the world.

THE MANE OF THE LION

All through
Days of summer
Like young cats rolling
Or swarms of painted Indians
We drank in a single season
The distillation of a lifetime.

Drunken hours hued
With apricots and clear champagne
Titanics unaware
That two sleepy lives
Were tangled
In the mane of the lion.

And like a startled deer
Caught in trellis patterns
Of afternoon sunlight,
The something
That we never named
Flinched and ran away.

PARALLELS

I remember . . .
We thought time slack
And young as we then;
We played an easy race
To show who loved the most —
Who had the best imagination;
New parallels of tenderness.
I remember skin —
Warm oranges in the sun —
Held tight,
Leaves in a pot
Pressing against summer
Windows for sunlight,
Sipping amber days.

Now extra skin shows
How lean is time
From racing, laughing;
Says there were many lost things;
Hurts and scars and such
Tended with growing age
In private gardens of hate.
Eyes — once burning glass —
Have grown sullen,
And all that's left
Is the sophistication of table salt.
Old parallels of compromise.
We hope with all our trinkets
To find peace and love in Hell.

IF THERE HAD BEEN A SON

A void of childlessness wonders
What might have been
The outcome of my blending,
Had there been the time
Of course.
Of course
There are too many now,
But then there always have been;
And my conceit surmounts
And hopes for the Exception.
Small soft hands and minds lost
Grow and find their way
Eventually . . .
But Age knows
Great things to teach,
And if there had been a son . . .

SANDRA L. HARDING

MONEY TALKS

A storm cracks the sky with a tight-lipped line of
      white-gray clouds.
The surf is split by the roar of the thunder.
The sea's response to the storm's fury?
— Waves that crest and foam . . .

Two men look to the sea and the storm.

A fisherman turns sail to harbor from emerald reefs.
He comes home awed by the sea's fury: knowing of
the sea's power; fearing for his boat and life.

A stockbroker at play resentfully folds his red and
orange umbrella, frowning at the gray skies;
no longer interested in the raging surf.

At dawn, the fisherman returns to the sea
To reap a full harvest from its cropland —
And finds a splintered dingy.

At dawn, the umbrella drifts back to the shore.
The stockbroker, who sneered, wings to New York
Untouched.

JAMES HARRER

W. W. ME

passion grated halfness
        away with time
the floor carried dust
balling for a kindly triune
        the unkept cobwebby corner
shudder

for swept as oft
        the shout careening
wall to wall
mirror to mirror
        hellion and cloud cover image
awake

tattle teller thirst
        crown bloody teeth
some extraneous extension
too real   all here
        find your mucous eyes
dead

call caller
        as if mental wretch
could make it so
lips parted muscle taut
        pull that self-made trigger
bang

ODE TO A SEARS-ROEBUCK CATALOG

a poet in silence be
waiting on the stair
if blood could mark it
    images up, off, away
        (so-so halls of mirrored glass shattered eternally)
           for fun — but not really
and this
        to all you bubble-gum hippies
that empty pattern can be so comfortable
    lest undiscovered oceans will not yet touch
    lest human circle remain

you see it all goes forth without you

HIROSHIMA

      flowing in some jagged state
          marks the illegible anxiety
bird runnings
        on a black sidewalk
              shaded bushes laugh at seared eyes
      scarred window wetness wrung from the blood
challenge from the sky
         this purple sun

      withering
      the zenith faints
    care gone there is thirst
        all steel roosters shall crow once more
here is truth

staring into each grapefruit death
         touching the hot fungus dead from the wave
             climbing above below above
        finds only this
      no water
         slop

    then the eternal aftermath
        a giant with his map hands out the offering
    some silly chocolate bar in its sterile foil wrap
        and
           a gorgeous mutation extends
its stubby bone
      thinking it's over
      this shiny reality of
      man and man

MICHAEL HARRIS

IN THE MOUNTAINS LOOKING FOR SOMEWHERE ELSE

we didn't like it,
just being there . . .
so we looked for somewhere else
to be amongst the pine needles,
juniper and fern,
foam in the creek,
the fly horde, chipmunks . . .
and when we found
that there wasn't anywhere else
to be but where we were:
we gave up the search
and went home.

FLORENCE HARTMANN

LOVE

The night was torn by the sounds of exquisite agony.
They felt the sadness of the forbidden rite.

His black body wracked with torment
    told her of the centuries of longing.
She was helpless.

As the night melted
They saw two strangers who knew the pain of forbidden love.

His body bore the marks of countless scars.
His eyes were sad.

She saw his soul.

LARRY HEACOCK

BLOWJOB

I see
as if
the wind finds meaning
in my face.

Weeds
pierce the white chapter
of my back,

the sky
is split in glaze of flesh
and angle.

Silent words,
the body favors motion
lost and sometimes
sorry.

I CANNOT FORGET

I cannot forget
the leopard sun
of my youth
that bent me back
into the tyranny
of the grass
and plagued the fever
of my days
with baseball.

I pretended
that Springtime
meant Freedom
when all the while
distant flowers
were laughing me
into their green beds
and speechless waters
held me swimming captive
in their wet jails.

I cannot forget
the sun that raced
my feet to the fields
and beat me
or how my shouts
would bounce
on the streets
into the grinning
afternoon.

And if I did forget,
forgiving these defeats,
I'm sure my life
would walk
with a too solemn grace
into a doomed
evening iced
with a western glow.

DESCENT AT 6 A.M.

A light
slashes his brain
with brilliance of
morning.

On a nervous
toilet he
sits risen from
the growling
bed.

The stairs have
rattled in
collapse
and the past
is at him
with orange
and flailing
tongues.

MARTHA HOCH

RECOLLECTION OF LOVE GONE

'Twas on a night like this, not long ago
        but long enough to make the wound bleed slower now,
I met him here and sat beside him, near enough to hear
        his heart beat, feel his breathing at my side,
Together, then, we spent the moments lost in thought,
        he, meditating closely at his papers,
        me, thinking only of my love for him,
More fleet than wings of hummingbirds, the days passed
        one on top the other, leaving for a trail
        the trace of summer winds that cooled his heart.

DAVID R. HOGG

CHRISTMAS EVE, 1965

a little man
an old man
hunches
crunches teeth against wind that lashes
wind that crashes,
spreading his coat
bat-like.

and he lunges
flying before the roar,
forcing chin on chest
trying to hide, to disappear.

later i see him
in an empty room
upsidedown
asleep.

AN ENCOUNTER DURING A WALK ALONG THE LAKESHORE

A child laughs in strong arms
And together they watch the sun die.
Feeling good, feeling safe as blackness rises around them.

Innocence tugging at his hand
To be carried on square shoulders,
Irresistible.
Warmth
Without sun's heat
In the tiny hand that pulls wind whipped hair
And whispers in spring's voice.

Down the quiet, darkening road they disappeared,
Blending slowly into night's pastels.

Nice, happy — I feel man's beauty,
Skip a stone on mirror water,
And go home.

EDMUND HOLMES

HAIKU

NOON-BRIGHT BRONZE

Lounging on his porch
At noon with his mug
        of beer —
Sun-warmth makes him drunk

        Wind-chimes tinkling
        After so long
                a silence —
        Shook by a fresh thought

81

Somewhere in this vale
After so long
     a gong
Tolls the sound of bronze

                  Old woman smoothing
                  The dirt around
                          her dahlias —
                  Mothering the earth

Jagged mountain ridge
Ripping through the light
     blue cloth
Cutting off her skirt

                  Shallow-breathing surf
                  Lulling on the beach
                        near by
                  Shall not wake his nap

Two men talking here
Not looking at each
     other
Sharing glancing thoughts

          UNALONE — THOUGHTS OF HER

Sleeping gray haired man
Unnoticed in the
     village —
Mountain in the mist

                  Alone — slackened mouth
                  Suddenly pulled up
                      at ends
                  By a jocund thought

Doves on the roof ledge
Ornament the line
     between
The house and the sky

                  The musicians string
                  Their cloth of mirth
                      together —
                  All of us can feel

Her body dances
To rhythms of
          the music —
Made physical song

                    Before that lithe girl
                    Passed me I was quite
                              content
                    Being all alone

Too many neat nymphs
Pass me without
          noticing
If I had seen them

FREEWAY AND FLYWAYS

Steel freeway girder
Spanning over city
          street
Framing future view

                    Concrete building form
                    Skeleton of its
                              future —
                    When it shall be razed

Like the minute hand
Progressing on its chart-
          route line
Speeding jet-thrust plane

                    Steel plane ascending
                    Into night time with
                              my love
                    Winks goodbye to me

Shadow on the earth
In the form of our
          island —
Cloud below this plane

Steel leviathan
Smoothly from the
        tarmac lifts
Upon its own gusts

In the bright blue air
Careening on the off-
        ramp —
Circle-gliding hawk

SPATTERS ON THE WINDSCREEN

Silent falling rain
Like thoughts before an
        action —
Seen unheard then splash

A gray sponge is wrung
Above our heads
        dripping wet —
Tropic twilight rain

Cold rock-garden bench
Slowly in the winter
        chill
Warming where I sit

Young sun after rain
No more afraid of
        dark days
Comes out of hiding

Welcome happy thought
Washing off these old worn
        cares —
Unexpected rain

Silently rain drops
Sprinkled from lead-
        heavy sky
Spatters the windscreen

That laughing sun-boy
Has been hiding for
        two days
Atop the gray roof

SNOW GROVE

Ecdysical trunk
Shards mist-licked
        shimmering blue —
Eucalyptus grove

Too soon out of sight
Sudden pleasures —flitting
        finch —
Smiling passing girl

Zig-zagging beetle
Crossing the blank
        white paper —
Skier on the slope

I have forgotten
The face of last
        winter's love —
It might keep me warm

When the clouds let up
The boughs were wearing
        rain drops —
Forest crystal beads

Snow pile on roof ledge
Dripping fresh water
        on slush —
Winter-formed fountain

Quick strokes of black ink
Reed sketched on gray
        rice paper —
Fir grove in the fog

THE SINAI WAR

Shuttering barren ground
  steel tank treads track
    continuously
Firing erect cannon
  full-gorged through
    charging thick-skin
Naked genitals
  sputtering
    black oil in
climax of masturbating war
  on the general's cap
    insignifying Horus-hawk
leading the campaign in
  consumating
    collapse
prostrate beneath
  devastation
    while above
mount on female form
  steel-skin smooth
    soars jacketed
hooded goggled warrior
  in prophylatic canopy with
    stick tumescent
from thumb press
  ejaculates
    fire-filling finality
into supine enemy
  lying across
    the necrophilic field

PAUL HOPPER

MOIST OF SOUL

Vaguest of all in a day of varied vagueness,
lying with a book on the couch after lunch,
pleasant in the very want of contour —
my nap until the cleaning women woke me;
or maybe it was I who cut it short,
anticipating their arrival in the room,
dispelling as they would the symptoms of vagueness;
or perhaps I had not even quite been sleeping,
but only under the illusion of it.

86

I picked up the book again when they entered the room,
and turned on my back, my head on the arm of the couch,
to read of working-class fecundity
and the complex uncertainty of population genetics,
due to the failure of certain characteristics
to be assignable to the simple action
of just a few independent genes;
and due to recessives possessing positive and negative
survival value at the same time.

MARY J. HUNTER

THE FEAR

hell is fantastic, a nightmare and madness;
its unbelievable pictures are infinitely alike:
expressing vivid sameness in frightening sights
and cries; it is not foreign or unknown.
hell has its gods in a magnificent card-board
box — and a red ribbon enfolds it so that it
lies too lovely to be opened.

these idols run fast and massive on a ball-
bearing plane with assembly-line workers of-
fering your face —
your ugly face — waving like a defective mind
in a glass window.
these worshippers are passive; they give up themselves for you. the vision of no one else is
too horrifying.
but if you mock them, your hands may grow heavy
with stones.

RANDALL JEWETT

THE WEB THEY SPIN

They never would ask me
how do I feel about it
maybe because they knew
I wasn't going to agree.
Our relations were suspended
in the most intricate web,
and my wise foolery precluded
a search that would have ended

in a way
to find my way
to its center.
O, but for me to say it out,
on my own,
would only show
the short cut
to there, and then
it would all be cut
and I could not get
back to "Start Here."

MARY JO JOHNSON

WALL HANGING

In this capture of the dead,
Standard color is the final insult,
Shaming the flames of candles lit
Beside tasteless tea unpoured;
Big keys dangling in static uproar
Around the smug-faced clock,
While it speaks softly of one-thirty's.

A room in time — freezing, frozen,
Where seasons fall backwards
And haunt one's sleeping mind;
The tug of age, descent of lines.

SAMUEL JOHNSON

ONLY IN AUTUMN

One day I saw it hanging there,
Glistening green.
Next day I saw it swinging there,
Without its sheen.
Another day I saw it fluttering there,
Red and orange tipped.
A later day I saw it withering there,
Curled up a bit.
That rare day I saw it dying there,
Now ugly and brown.
The last day I saw its ending there,
Crumpled on the ground.

C. MICHAEL JONES

OH PERPETUAL ANXIETY

oh perpetual anxiety —

        hunger of the flesh
     waiting for the improbable

   stop
      a foolish cry

   oh help me
          i pain
               i hurt
   why this senseless lingering
wait
   for what

the inner throb
          the soul writhes
          the mind tires
   but no sleep — think think think
                  greater pain

   a cold walk
         no help
   fresh air
      still none

a loud trio adds to the grey sediment
   the brain sinks into a knot
   a lonely light or two begging for company
     and yet repulsing it

a haunting face
        a cold hand on warm feet
   sandals for your hair

   away
     out
       gone
   but not quite
back again to quick incongruous rhythm

oh love — change

POET-MAN

Poet-man
don't leave now
stay
and tell me
how to see
and what will come
tomorrow
and who will know me
then
and what is love
oh poet-man
and what is love
and show me
how to hear
the coocoo's call
and go
and know
and not return
but ever travel
with the wind
and past the sea
and through the trees
the forests
of my mind
the eye
of yesterday
never to be heard
or seen
or cared about
by other than
another poet-man
a prophet
left to wander
like yourself
forever
through a ruined castle
hiding ghosts
or lovers' vows
with graphic lines
of shaded spires
and tumbled bricks
and wearied words
of long-dead poems
never
to be read again

but stored
for children
to pass on
and never give
a second thought
but for old time's sake
the faded pictures
bound to stay
will never live
again
but die
and tell
a classic story
of a long-dead
poet-man
a brother
born to lead the poor
through deserts
hot with flaming tongues
the tongues
of satan's band
that tempt the soul
and rust
the mind
and kill the priests
then leave
and not be held
in check
but free
to come and go
and tease the senses
always
to remain
a home
for travelers
of barren lands
the lands
that hold the castles
hiding ghosts
and waiting
waiting still
for jailers to unlock
the doors
and free at noon
the hands that give
immortal words
to me

oh poet-man
don't leave now
stay
and tell me
how to see.

YOU ARE A WORD

you are a word
more
an experience
that you will not admit
you know me
and yet
you are afraid
afraid
to care too much
for anything
that might get hurt
always fading
peace
leaves a corner empty
and destined
never to be filled
smiles
are fleeting images
formed
from what you feel
unsure
afraid
but never gone
always faith
and love
will cry out
to shape your
world
not a world
of non-significance
but real
alive
and you can see
realize
that —
you
can see
and ebbing pain

of yesterdays
is forgotten
for today
but still
the word remains
your word
and you cannot
escape

beauty

MARGARET A. JONES

MAD . . . SONG

"The rent's due," she said
and loosed the rats again
"#371?"   I said
to the church
where the green-slatted shutters
banged in early evening
behind the blue dark
spruce trees on the lawn

She came.   And we
left
and again the rats ate
what was left of my mother-in-law's
purple rice

and the refrigerator has more black fingerprints on it
from where the man came to fix
the linoleum   again
but left   a yardstick   standing
by the wall

and the shutters creak
beyond the blind
lets in a dirty
box of beige light

"The rent's due," she said
"#372?"   I said
and loosed the rats   myself
   just to show
I too   could play
the
   game

93

AMERICAN DEATH

                    Last night:
a prisoner-of-war camp
where American women
and children
were let to   run   loose

blue floodlights

over a spring field
in front of a Greek

church   where red tulips

by   wooden steps

to run free   in front
of pleasure-seekers   masses
whose automobiles   were to
race us to   death
force   us   forward
like   deer   and   fawns
                    before a wave of fire

those steel painted faces
grimaced   in ecstacy
as machines   tore
                    flesh
tossed   it
on the field

and my sister   was found

smothered
        under a ripped
mattress   feathers strangling

and the keepers
did not even think to pry
the gravel from her back
before
        pushing
            her
pressed body   into
                the burial pit

1963

One day of sun,   or mist
brings memories of other   days
like it,   and moist   cold
grass   and wild onions,
or the shallow tinkling cough
of children:
icy water in a tankard
with one   March shadow,   sunlight
hour in that Spring:

MOUNTAIN

Bright thin late-day light
                breaks
transparent shadows over   mountain quartz
                        reflecting

crevice edges
            and bright clumps
                        scattered
            wet wildflowers

yellow
        in arctic alpine willows
        in tundra growth
mountain pebbles   hold
a cosmos
        garden
tiny lakes
and   blue spruced   snow
reflect   the dying suns

THE FRUIT PICKERS
from photographs by Dorothea Lange

We watched the dark fruit trees,
                    the sun sank behind them
and sat on the grass
moist   evening cool   comes with the sun going
round   full golden   mythical   apple
down full of silence

Shadow reached for the fruit
turned it gray in the twilight   tissued by birdsong
            bob o'link sounds
larks from the fields
round and round us the winds

95

and around us the grass
beyond us the fire
we lay down and slept

MORRIS S. JORDAN

THE QUEST

For though my master led me through my hell
   And helped me bear the untold psychic pain,
      I knew his bounds were in the Bleak One's reign —
But ghostly thoughts drove on my mortal shell.
I begg'd that he those heinous shades dispel:
   With one swift purge relieve my Ixion brain
      Or ever damn me to a world profane —
For me resound that fateful, summ'ning knell!

Then how my heart leapt up when I beheld
   My Beatrice come to make this dark soul blest!
      Divinely graced, she flashed her heav'n-hued eyes
To bid me kneel to Love, and thus enfold
   To me the longed-for object of my quest,
      The lily and roseate patterns of Paradise.

DEATH

Death is the call of the watch to tumble aloft,
And, still alert, the seaman-soul sways above,
Clinging with exhilarated tenacity 'twixt heav'n and earth
At the topmast head.   He sways through the sky,
Inspiring the ethereal air and observing closely
The mundane matters of the compact world below.
Clearly discerning now,   and yet merging them,
The assimilator himself,
            the free-but-clinging soul
Knows now the truth,
            the complete intellectual bond
Between the Spirits of heaven and the Business of earth,

And with true philosophy
        (too late)
           now sails on

    eternally

96

THE SOUL'S AGONY

Disappointment . . . Disillusionment . . . Embitterment . . .
From its lowest depths, the soul cringes,
Then ruptures forth in rebellion, but,
Crushed by its own empty agony,
Cries forth a low note,
A growl that crescendoes into a veritable scream,
Which echoes among the cold, stark headlands,
The pristine peaks, and the jutting crags.
It jars the avalanches; they slide down in torrents:
Off comes the cornice, silently slipping through cold, bleak space
Until the impact and explosion on the chill downs below.

. . . Onward through the peaks winds the weary wail,
Now a shriek, now a moan, now a sob
Rivalling the anguished cries of the alpine storms
In its savagely impassioned intensity.
Upward, upward towards the blue
The rueful chord explodes,
An ever mournful, ever mounting shade
That ceases not its soul-rending All-Erebean wails until
It presents its private hell before that gate on high,
Before the domain of the cruel Author of All Fate.
Back and forth, 'twixt hell and high gate
It echoes: unceasing, rebounding, nerve-tearing.

Then the fog rolls in: The gray, swirling mists
Surround the crags and slide into the valleys.
It dims, darkens, dulls, muffles.
The mouth of the cave, the doorway to Hell,
Becomes dark, and even the cries emitted therefrom
Cannot penetrate the bleak wall.
Even the fiery sign of "Abandon Hope
Ye Who Enter Here," is obscured,
And a numbing, an absence, suddenly
Jerks into the breast. The fog . . .
Bleak, indistinct, nothing but a blank mass,
A dank mass, a throttling vapor
That catches the sound and vaporizes it, too.

A single flash, then gray again.
"Abandon Hope," in its grimness, had flickered once again.
Now not even that moan of bitter anguish can be heard.
The numbing of the miasmic fog is killing it.
The macro-cosmic struggle now shaking the breast
Is dying. The voluminous internal shriek
Passes into oblivion. Inside it is dark.
The oblivion admits a low moan, then a whimper,
Then . . . nothing.

MICHAEL KATZ

I SAND

I shift with the hot wind;
Tumble and flow into dry rifts.
Swirling I,
            over around between
                        parched plants
Suffocating the tired, dragging wanderer,
Cracking his lips and gritting his rasp
And
Cough.

The afternoon flames and scorches on
But I am one with a dull heat
                        and heat
                              and heat . . .

Slowly the dying sun glows red and dims in the fading distance.
The sting of ice is in the air.
Overhead a white star pierces the fast darkening sky.

        . . . a dull heat
                  and warm
                        and Cold.

Bleak freezing wind whips dunes into a rigid formation —
I stare inward at
Cold
Clammy
Dirt.
I see the harsh white moon of snow
Cut away stark cliffs.

The shivering grasses cringe
At my touch
The weary stranger cries.

HARRIET OXFORD KIDD

        They introduced you to me
            And I heard you say
        In your quiet casual way
            Oh, we've met.
        You did not betray by word
            Those hours, our hours,
        That eternity of love.
            But I watched the silent sorrow
        Of your smile and felt again
            Your heart on mine.

They did not know that introduction
    Brought such pain.
We'll likely meet another day
    Yet, we've met, is all we'll say.

ANDREW MacTEARLACH KINNAIRD

THE WAY OF THE CROSS

The Voice of Christ: "I am the Door!
    I live, though once I died.
And behold, I live for evermore
      That the Gates of Life might open wide
        Upon the straight and narrow road —
        The path that the Suffering Servant trod
        That leads to the very throne of God.
    And I am the Master Guide.
"My blood, unpriced, was poured out as dross
    On Golgotha's curséd tree.
        I am the Way, the Truth, the Life,
        The Path of trial, with dangers rife;
For the way of the Christ is the way of the cross.
      Come! Suffer and die with Me."
Yes! Here is the Way, the way to the crown:
The way of the cross, and the life laid down
      On the altar of the Lord.
For the corn of wheat must die to live,
And the only true life is the life He will give;
      But the Way is long and hard.
"The Way is too long and too hard," said Man,
    "And traversed now by few.
        A smooth side road is the kind we need,
        And a smooth wide road we shall have indeed
For we'll draw up a master plan
    And blast a highway through."
Thus, they constructed it firm and broad
    And smooth as a sheet of glass.
        And wide the acceptance, and great the acclaim
        For the highway that went under Jesus's name.
Convenient and pleasant, the road
    Of the Christ without the cross.
Some walked this road for commercial gains,
    And some their prestige to display.
      But the Christ of God
      Wept tears of blood
    For their hearts were far away.

And some clapped their hands, shouting "Jesus saves!
    And He keeps from day to day."
      "Oh why," said the Word,
      "Do they call me Lord
    And do not the things I say?"

"Yes! Why do they call Him Lord," said Man,
    "And do not His words obey?
      His words are true and wise and good —
      We'll shoulder the cross and we'll pour out *our* blood
Let the future be *ours* to plan!
    The cost we will gladly pay."

Thus, a new road was built by the children of want
    Over hunger and poverty gross;
      For men who had taught them that Jesus saves
      Had oppressed and exploited and worked them like slaves.
Disowning a Church of cant,
    They followed the way of the cross.

To the true narrow way o'er mire and moss
    And mountain and crag, two roads were spliced:
The way of the Christ without the cross,
    And the way of the cross without the Christ.

The proud and the rich in these lands we call "Free"
    Use the highway that bears Jesus' name,
While the Communist masses have shouldered the tree
    And hope, through its sacrifice, claim.

For the man that would tread the path of the cross
    May meet the Christ on the way.
      But what of the man who bears His name
      And none of the sacrifice, suff'ring and shame?
What glories of earth can stone for the loss
    Of the light of eternal day?

The Voice of Christ: "Behold I come
    As the thief that comes by night.
Let all the tongues of Man be dumb!
    Shall not the Judge of all do right?
      I am not mocked. As you sow, you shall reap.
      Then work in my vineyard and do not sleep.
      For blessed, at My coming, My servants that keep
My commandments and walk in the Light.

"For My blood unpriced, was poured out as dross
    On Golgotha's curséd tree
      I am the Way, the Truth, the Life,
      The Path of trial with dangers rife;
For the way of the Christ is the way of the cross.
    Come! Suffer and die with Me."

NATURAL CHILDBIRTH

The savage squats upon the earth,
And quickly, painlessly gives birth.
She scant appreciates the worth
    Of anaesthetics, drugs and such
    As we have come to need so much.

ARTHUR KINSEY

A PROGRESSION IN COINCIDENCES OF DOUBLETHOUGHT

Lost in great high tombs
Can only man ever stay.
To offer
To his everlasting
Love only nihilation, even lost yet.
In nescience
Springs, pure in rite, inward teachings.

Lots of nothing everywhere. Look inward. Nothing—ever so stable.
Does onlyness ever stop?
Nihilation of time
May even allow nescience
To heal everything.
All beings seat, egocentrically, negations capable, easily
Of furthering
Obsolete meanings.

In the state
Of negation lands your
Theme, hovering, ever
Still, to attempt ryhming the
 Only form
Used never in themes years
Wore in the happy
Illegitimate near failure idle notes in the yore.

Wonderment has ever negated
Only mere
Happenings and states.
Clearness, only, may ever
Tell how each
Lucid *I* goes higher to
Hear all sounds.
People inhale each reality closed ever dimly
To his eagerness.
Vainly, each inward looks.
Only from
Universal nurturing, knowledge nears our wandering ignorant
                    nihilated goals.

JOHN EDWARD KIRCHHOFF

WHAT QUESTION — THE ANSWER

When's the right time,
   is now the time
   or never the time.

What's the concern?
   it's you the concern
   no It's the concern?

Is everything good
   or good everything, or anything.
   it's all good
   nothing bad is good or good bad?

Is this the answer or
   nothing the answer?
   But we're the answer
   or
   It the answer?

Is it they, or It, what is,
   and us whom it isn't
   or is neither It?
which is it!

Is what is, is right? or right it is,
   is It?

Is I thou or thou I
   No it isn't, is it?

Can it be said
   who is dead who is free?
   maybe red!

Is dead free
   and free dead, and never?
   Seem both it does,
      doesn't it?
Are you it or is it you?

Equal isn't equal
   not equal
   is equal.

It's black and white. Right white!
   White right?
     Neither is both
      both is neither.

moral is immoral
 immoral is moral.

God was
Man is
God is
 is man?

JOHN KOCAK, JR.

VIDEO TAPE REPLAY

 woke up
to find myself half-way in the world.
the sun was so bright that
i had to close my eyeshades to see blood-red.
i thought of many things in microseconds, ah.

 dragged my way downstairs,
i guess it was thoughts of overnight-longed food.
 it sufficed.

 found the way to work
(noticed the regular people-faced incidents).
 greet your boss with a smile,
a bit strained at that.
 now i work for my rest.

 the noonhour greets me with a gasp.
i gobble fooood down my gullet like a Southern slave.
music infiltrates my receiving membranes,
which are lost in the sound of crunching fooood.
militarily went back to work.
 aye, aye, sir.

 five hours A.L. (After Lunch),
completed my trivial work & went to the john.
 left my job,
the United Network to Keep the Poor Occupied,
to go home.

 sung songs to myself as i walked . . .
 ''with tangerine trees and
 marmalade skies . . . '',
 ''doing the garden, digging
 the weeds, who could ask for
 more . . . ''.

                              o,
how my ambulators tingle with over-distance.
                    there they are!
workers of the Race unite & u'll get home.
that's one Race that's free.

                    de-energized,
i sit at my residence with paper & clean hands,
ready for tomorrow's playback of today.
                    i yawn to sleep.

                —— PEOPLE

         We had our prohibition people
         and now it's changed,
         jiggled, squeezed and rearranged
                    to
         edsullivan people.

         Performances are produced
         daily and nightly, prayer-like.
         Convulsively, the mind is lost
                    in
         elvispresley movements.

         What's to come? What's gone?
         Analysts can't say; nor
         arthurclarke people either.
         "Maybes" best describe it all;
                    until
         , the jesuschrist people come.

PAUL J. KOCAK

                THE 84th TO 86th DAY
(an unDangling Conversation . . . with apologies to Paul Simon)
                to Mary Ann

         It's just 'round midnight words we shared —
         it being after tea.
         'twas Jasmine tea and jug band tunes.
         Our hearts we spoke and i'e we bared.

         Your lips, the morning's dew, 'pon mine.
         It's morn. Must leave your face.
         We bid "good night" at such a time
         when morning's just the same.

                    104

Remember When   that game we played.
And even now   a while.
We travelled here to there   to play
to walk   to hear our smiles.

But now I'm here and you are there
and love is where we are.
We'll cherish now as much as there
before me now you are.

THE DEATH SONG OF THE EASTER – MELILOT
or MARY ANN'S SONG OF BIRTH

    Easterflowers, heavenwhite tides, and shiny times
    are the images you cast –
    are the images that last.

Now a sonorant, mild melilot is singing to me:
"Remember when her voice first paused your mind?"
"Yes, it was just a year ago," said I.
"Remember when her face first rained sunshine?"
"Yes, that was a year ago too," I replied.
"And remember the times of holding hands?"
"Yes, sweet clover, I still delight in all that."

    Easterflowers, heavenwhite tides, and shiny times
    are the images you cast –
    are the images that last.

Again, the sonorant, mild melilot sung me:
"And since then, have you forgotten her?"
"No, my dear clover, how could I ever?"
Then, with a smile, poor melilot vanished.
"Easter-melilot, now where have you gone?"
And I could not find her anywhere   until
the sonorant voice of a girl sung with me:

    "Easterflowers, heavenwhite tides, and shiny times
    are the images you cast –
    are the images that last

    may they ever last . . . "

YVES HENRI LACAZE

SHADED LIGHT

I love the song of a negro, the last
shaded light of the freeman's beacon,
Requiem to a blemished past, the brand
of white irons on a flouted back.
I love the tones that spring forth
from this black string of God's violin,
The ancient tune it plays, a tell-tale
clue to the mystery of a harassed race —
Children playing hide and seek
in the darkness of their skin.
I love his ballad about a thousand slaves
airing the boudoir of an Egyptian queen.
I love his prayer in the sunlight
of an African day,
Where the sun shines for the white man
behind the temple door,
But shades its light for the black man
singing on the good earth's floor!

OSCEOLA

You were the sinewy limbs, proud and firm,
    of our first American.
You were the eagle-eyes that searched the jungle
    and the plain
For the hidden cotton-mouth and the treacherous
    swamp,
The lean, hungry mountain lion, the ever present
    menace of the white man.

You were Osceola, the untamed, with the kinship
    of the chieftain in your veins —
Chief of the Seminoles when the arrow and
    the battle-ax
Were the emblems of war and the symbol of grief.
You were the blood-brother to the Greeks,
    who ventured to Florida-land
In pursuit of the grace of your gods, of cool
    lakes and an evergreen glade.

You were the defiant Indian brace who dared
    to dip
Your arrows in the wounds of the paleface,
And penned a leaf in the history of your
    stalwart race.
You were Osceola, a god among men, whose faithful
    were exiled but faced it with strength.

Today, they are *blanket Indians*, your valiants
    of yore,
In the land of your gods, the evergreen glade
    and the jungle of Seminole lore —
The last living monument to your kingly origin,
    a spirit once blazing, a portrait now fading
Of the glorious legend of the vanishing American!

KATHRYN LANDSIEDEL

FOR SALVADOR

Sharing a theme, laughing in sunshine,
        Carnations, rum-water, Purua.
Caring together, sailing til dusktime,
        Bright'ning the shade of Aquila.

    A shadow walked the beach of Acapulco.

Taxco in June days, Cathedrals in gold,
        Winged Victory approving a chance.
Roaming through Londres, Genoa, Reforma,
        Pathways of circumstance.

    A shadow walked the beach of Acapulco.

A smile unopened, a look drowning,
        Warm flesh, warm moon, warm sand.
A poem belonging, hands closing,
        Soft voice, soft sea, soft land.

    My love walked the beach of Acapulco.

Glances in mirror, my name in accent,
        Study in heart — I need you.
Promises whispered, gentleness melting,
        Touch of my palm, night-dew.

    A shadow; Mi Amor.

107

POST TO GIA LONG

The end came on white wings, not silver, not blue,
With triangular knots of despair.
Speak no more my friend, don't utter the hard parallels
Reaching a gnarled neverness on a thoroughfare where few,
   Few I say on a wage of daring,
   Expecting an echoed retort . . .

But enough. May galloped across his back
On soft-fingered sighs of gratitude.
Imprinted love not to be forgotten,
Nor Sabres flashing through skies tracked on an ebon mecca
   Divided by singular drops of time.

Come fortnight, swiftly. Seal mine eyes awhile,
To open again only on intransigent skyscrapers
And concrete people lost in a file
Of indifference.

SANDERS ANNE LAUBENTHAL

WIND

From the window of my bitter spouse
I lean, tasting the light wind from the north,
Forgetting him dim below in the silent house
Brooding at table, forgetting my old vows,
Hearing the voice of the other call me forth.

He offers me sun-drenched clouds and careless noons
On river isles, symphonies, chandeliers,
Picnics in spring and hyacinths under moons,
While here I sweep bare pine floors and wash tin spoons
And the salt south wind blows sand down the wearing years.

Shall I not divorce this dragger who sits below,
Whose black hair straggles his brow, whose eyes are blind
As grey seas with fruitless vision, who
Compels me to bare toil — or even now
Pay mind to words we loosed on the sea wind?

108

ELEGY FOR A PRINCESS

Anna Maria Bittel Laubenthal
March 23, 1883 — January 7, 1967

Eyes that gaze at you out of an old face,
Pools of brown light, watchful and wise
— In a nameless Frenchwoman's portrait in the greys
Of the Delgado gallery, and her eyes
At Thanksgiving in the spiderless dim room
Where peacock feathers bloomed by her curled grey hair
As she talked to Kenny Fann, weighed him as groom
For a granddaughter prophesied as bachelor.

Christmas found her in snows of sterile sheets;
In corners lurked tubes like tentative spider-thread.
The red paper bell on the wall was a deceit
We put there to scare the lurkers from her bed;
Little Cathy, gift-like in red dotted-swiss,
With Christmas-bowed soft hair, was another. We
Were still in fealty though to the weakened voice
And knelt at command for antiphoned rosary.

At New Year's dusk we tiptoed into the room,
In our bright clothes that greyed in the ashen glow
Of the last lamp. Emboldened in the gloom,
The noiseless threads had curled out and below,
Snaring the lioness. In a tangle of tube
She lay unmoved; their weird pale colors crept
Round her like giant webs in a cramped mirkwood.
The spiders had been. Bitten, unconscious, she slept.

On the octave day, I sprang to the strident phone
With the news known before I raised a hand.
Southward beyond cold miles, poison had won.
A lost house speaking German, sand in the wind;
Sand the designer she sewed for, sand the fox
In Sunflower woods, old roses turret-hung.
But her brow said no. Unreal in the wreathed box,
She had broken away from the spiders and grown young.

MARCHERS IN THE DARK

The loud indistinct cry
Coming from distance, rhythmic, repeated, harsh;
Marchers stamping by
In the dark outside the Italianate dim church,

Unseen, sinister,
Identity lost in the deep, close-wrapping night,
Presage of the hour
When the last peace will drown in the shout of might.

ABSTRACT

I have lost even the memory of your face.
Grey eyes I remember, hair darker than trees
Leaning at dusk over chopped seas to embrace
A tempestuous sunset. Naming over these,
I am left with a faceless abstract, a thin wraith
That vanishes when I call it by your name.
Or am I myself the phantom, keeping faith
Barely, a match-smoke riven from its flame?

Your absence makes me this ghost, this undead,
That moves like a perfect robot through a waste
Of stagnant waters. It smiles, moves, nods its head,
Tinkling a music-box tune, cameo-faced.
But it has neither joy, nor heart, nor thought
Till you come back, whose loss all this has wrought.

DAVID LAWSON

PORTRAITS

I

In the neighborhoods
Of our lives there stand
Houses and memories of houses,
Fragmented locations
Dispatched from sleep,
Inward beckonings
From somewhere into nowhere,
Forgetful as a purpose vanishing
Through doorways opened
On a page of night.

Here stand the porticos
From which to hold
This tryst of dislocation,
The rooms for drawing
Shutters on our losses;
There the evocations,
Dreams and readings,
Reliquaries of a day
Outnumbered, a mythos
For our spent devotions.

110

II

In your presence,
That October afternoon,
I sensed your quiet
Minnesota roots,
Calm sisterhood of trees,
The graces of America,
A brown, still house,
Bay windows fronting shrubbery,
Rooms filled with Brahms
In winter listenings.

Your face disclosed
Reflections of this land,
And I,
Your momentary prisoner,
Made free to roam
Upon those whispering years,
Touching truth
Where sky and grasses blend,
Sighted your home
On horizontal hills.

III

Straddling a jutting cliff
Of prose she writes
On clouds: some absurd girl,
Mumbling awkward logic,
Strides backwards
Into dusk on flowing hair
With childhood notebooks
Flung in disarray,
Their words as flashbacks
Gone to fetch the skies.

She is pursuing the identity
Of buried trees, and also sings
Of horses' manes, lost roots,
Whiskered men at war with enemies:
Fancied years when time
(Then dwelling near the tide
In hidden boats) would clasp
Forgotten hands, drawing her essence
Down into a verbal tangle
From the past, a web of lasting days.

111

IV

Risking the loss
Of April doves
And other trespassers
Upon our days
We plot untrodden poems;
Siblings to shadows,
We structure lyrics
After sudden elms
Or flower-beds hoed
By shapers of bright sequences

In the summer substance
Of their certitude;
And riven with the peril dreamed,
Make combat with lions
Through gardens growing
Inauthentic as imagined deeds.
Here in this dark,
Impalpable chronology,
Where time and thunder stalk,
No image of reality prevails.

JOHN ALAN LETSINGER

SONNET

A tree, like memory, puts forth its leaves
From loam of yesterday's most precious flowers;
From musty leavings of the past, concieves
The shimmerness of Springtime's sweetest hours.
The poet-lover hoards his hours of bliss;
He coffers each caress against that frost
Which brings, perforce, surcease of happiness:
That, even at Love's death, no memory is lost.
When after-tears have washed the face of pain,
And gentle Time, in time, soothed bitter loss,
The singer, then, will to the song again
To hush the breath of gods with his disclose.
Thus, though from love, love oftentimes declines,
The Songs of Loss the loss oft far outshines.

THEY

The incredible passage
Of clowded brows and misted orbs
That come before these argus eyes
Every passing breeze
Wafts the smoke of exotic flowers,
Of bleedings wrists
Of burning eyes
Of foliage slightly bruised by love,
Or only slightly;
Ah, how impressive
These false crystals
Of loves that were never near to love—
That said nothing
Between the brushing of the lips —
Whose bodies only spoke
The language of the hair and the eyeshadowed eye.
These false crystals
Wept from eyes
That knew naught but the shallowness
Of joy and pain;
These scrall-crossed faces,
Youth-abandoned long ago . . .
Oh, faces, hid in mist,
Voices muffled by Time's lost hour,
You expound the ugliness of death,
But not only:
The lost and undersea hearts,
The tortured and unfeeling eyes
That feel too keen
That ache between the thighs,
That long to drink
The poetry of ripened pears;
These play eternal games
And whisper secrets that they think are new
To the Modern Pitheus
Or current Phaedrus.
Hesitating, the brush of Time
Strokes on the drop of change.
Time's efforts fail;
Only players change,
The set remains the same.

SONNET

A million words each single Muse could teach,
And shew an hundred ways to say each phrase.
But, when with pen a lonely man does reach
And try to capture stars in his dim praise —
The he do fail to light with life and sky —
Perhaps, in Art, he shares their dignity.
The poems that my Muse dictates to me
Can be but shadows of that which I feel.
Can Man, in mirrors of a language see
The Spirit that was once alive and real.
The artist is compelled to sing, and sing he must
To save some part of that which is but dust.
And all of Art is but a simple prayer
That time, in some small part, might beauty spare.

GEORGE H. LEWIS

ON MARGATE SANDS

I

Tiresias in the yellow tent
Leaves coke bottles where they lay
Giggles his heels at ignorance
And then begins to pray.

And all the lone-sound sailors
Are screaming — they all know
That cross-iron kisses on the run
Have cast them down below.

And Wind twists round the screaming trees
It huddles, afraid to blow
The yellowed papers from the streets,
The sand across the show.

II

The black parrot tells the captain
Which way the waters flow;
And how a local loser walked
On them a while ago —

A friend of Pocahontas, who
Without his water wings
Was put into the circus
And billed the king of kings.

114

The captain laughed and scratched his nose
An iceberg hove in view;
He stepped into the water
Though he forgot his crew.

III

The Moor is washing dishes
In the cafe on the hill;
He thinks he won't kill mamma
But the dwarfs all know he will

It's sad to see him blow his mind
And turn to her in pain;
He stumbles through the door and drives
Around the block again.

The circus lights are winking red
Like blood seen through the rain;
De Salvo of the world is dead;
The dwarfs were all insane.

IV

The riverbank, the circus dump
Hears humming on the air;
Ophelia with her folk guitar
Is stroking out a prayer.

And all sailors who come ashore
Transform themselves to pigs;
Ophelia with the gentle hands
Builds castles out of twigs.

The river calls, she holds a tune
And hums it far below;
A current parts her gown at last;
Picked bones begin to show.

V

The river's tent is burning now;
The yellow sound of Wind
Is filling up the ice-cream sky
With blackened shreds of skin.

The hanged man blindly stumbles forth
And with no protocol
He sadly begins carving
His face into the wall.

Smoke is snuggling round his eyes
He stumbles to his knees
And chews a couple credit cards
Then flies into the trees.

VI

And all great men are swarming
Mutely to the bay;
Satisfied there's nothing left —
Left nothing there to say.

And Cortez and Balboa
Are tripping through the rain;
With handbags full of petty cash
From their last big trip to Spain.

As pale circles of the storm-tossed moon
Slide east on seas that glow;
Death and the raven drift above
The strawberry side show.

K. DANNA LINFOOT

SITTING ON A HILLSIDE, STUDYING LIFE

Many a boy his age is elsewhere now
(cheating on a test or driving fast),
but he's a pensive creature, quite alone
sitting on a hillside, studying life.
A soaring eagle seems to rest in flight,
circling over small and easy prey;
bustling rodents chatter and ignore
the predatory form that looms above.
The boy, to end the suspenseful death-scene,
raises his .22 and shoots two women
in an approaching Ford.

DEATH-WISH OF TOO MUCH LOVE

Sometime I will fly away alone
On wings whose rushing beat will melt the bone.
To sure aloneness, but to surer soul:
Not forced to grapple with a two-heart role,

For standing here —

the tumult in my mind
and the witch-brew in my heart
and the vile words so near escape
from lips that wish to kiss instead of curse —

I see you both and wish myself away:
A better-dead than hotly-severed heart.

116

THE BRINK

The brink of day —
I blink, I sleep.

The brink of life —
I blink, I die.

    Lights and smiles turn off   and on   and off:

    The lids of my paperweight eyes
                jump
                  away

From the pull of Hell
Like virgin feet on a
          sunken
              coal
                bed.

TERRENCE LISBETH

LEHENGRIN

Rendered the earth, stellar
circumscription, sunknight
swanning whiteness
from the darkly pensive,
the shining grail.

Skythunder Odin the mind
of Ortrud, the destruction
of sacramental joining.
Nocturnal procession —
sword death (for mystery),
godly brother from swan ashes risen,
the dove to the passing of
Lehengrin's love.

JOAN DEE LOEB

WHO AM I

I am for the first time
A woman
Young, Vibrant, Alive;
No longer the child of yesterday's sorrows.

117

I am ready for life
Not afraid
No longer searching;
My direction has been sighted.

I am unclassified
Untyped
Arty, Feminine, Impulsive;
Each is part of the unique me.

I am more than that
All me
A little of a lot;
Dabbling in the Art of Life.

THE PEDESTAL

I

He stood atop the pedestal.
The sign said, "fragile, handle with care,"
So I did
Until time began
To wear upon this fine pedestal
And the base began to weaken.
A strong wind came and
Dislodged a stone,
Then a careless bypasser
leaned upon the tattered remains —
They fell and scattered.
There he stood
Upon the ground
Alone, unsupported by the pedestal.
I walked away.

II

Broken, scattered, the pedestal had lain
As time passed until
I came that way again.
He stood upon the ground still
And watched
As I picked up the broken remains
To build a new pedestal,
Higher and stronger.
No warning to take care was needed
For it was carved of marble
And could not be destroyed by time.
I would walk away again
Leaving him upon the pedestal
For the dealer of Art
Who could pay the price for such near perfection.

SANDPIPER

I sit upon the rock
Watching —
As the Sandpiper rushes
Like a small child to a circus
Toward the water's edge.

Searching for life's gift
Afraid —
Running eagerly forward,
But retreating as the sea moves
Toward his small feet.

Not knowing quite what it means.

Fear neither the salt or the foam,
The sea will fulfill you.
Be open and unafraid
As the sea is open and unafraid.

I sit upon the rock
Watching —
As the sandpiper rushes
Like a small child to a circus
Toward the water's edge.

WILLIAM E. LOVELY

Smoke, Fire, Ashes, Dust
what else have I or who
to trust — my loved one
has left for journey
long — a trip of
friendships weak and
strong — love was
one sided, oh yes I knew but
cared not I nor would you for if
you could but see
(her tender smile and eyes of brown)
your heart as mine would
jump and bound.
Her trip will last I
hope not long, for
I'm still here and
I sing love's song, and I'll
carry the torch of love for her
deep down in heart forevermore.

WILLIAM M. MAGRUN

RAGE TO LIVE

The rage to live like a weeping willow,
    never straying from its ground;
Bends to the burdens of its love,
    and whispers nary a single sound.

It casts its shade with loving care,
    protects from sun and rain;
While in the night it stands alone,
    and shivers in the wind with pain.

Weather mocks its strength with age,
    but the willow's roots hold fast,
To greet the sun's first golden strands,
    and once again its love to cast.

And when the willow greys with years,
    and its roots begin to slip,
Who is there to give it thanks,
    who is there for it to grip?

The weeping willow sheds its tears,
    and bears its burden brave;
Such fools who never realize,
    they've lived their lives in vain.

WHAT WORTH WHEN?

To find and accept happiness, just for an instant,
is to accept agony forever;
    But what worth when?
        or dream forever.

Salvation is the death of the instance,
and the birth of agony, almost regrets;
    But what worth when?
        or dream forever.

Love is victory in battle but defeat in war,
and the enemy, the dream, that wins by its own defeat;
    But what worth when?
        or dream forever.

For is one moment of happiness worth a lifetime of
dreams, or is the agony of defeat from victory too
much to bear, and the hope of a dream enough?
    For dream forever, or dream no more.

JOHN THOMAS MANNING

THE GRAND AND GLORIOUS HOLY WAR
or NECTAR SOURED

Islam waged a bloody reign
To spread the Spirit
Yet she failed.
For
Men do not carry their hearts
In their hands.

True, the Sacred Kaaba
Held her skirts about her wide
And minarets sprang from forts:
Islam's might gleamed steel:
Yet the Spirit cried:

> Men cannot *wage* the holy Faith
> For hearts and souls are not so won!
> Set forth the Faith like birds to flight
> And reap the gleaming harvest-pearls.

>> Birds caged are dead
>> How golden though the seed:
>> Lotus forced is nectar soured.

> The gusted breath of choice
> Shall set them to the fields!
> Whose eye is clear
> Shall get the grain (and win the granary!)
> Whose eye is clouded with himself
> Shall go for chaff
> And get it.

The ancient minarets arose
Yet crumbled all within
For the imperial boot of thousands chanting
    Allah, Lord!
Rings only in the ears of men
    And for what are ears
    But dust, decay?
What sings within the hearts of men
Rings only to the Lord of Winds.

So, too, men cannot *wage* a peace
No matter how noble, golden, true.
Free peace as the bird to flight;
Leave your swords (rifles, gas, napalm bombs and Hueys);
Embrace your brother: Love him well.
And harvest all the pearls.

121

ON CONSEQUENCE

I picked a white lilac today:

The first on Spring
The frogs do sing.

While all about the
Things of Consequence bellowed,
Shrieked a shrill of ideologies,
Groaned of children dying, starving,
trampled by the insane armies:
Faceless causes: Faceful men.

About again the melody strengthens
And I turn in nausea to lilacs:

Oh do not say man is unfeeling!
But overmuch he feels the horror
And cannot tell.

In face of so much Consequence
Only inconsequent is Consequent.

HILLS' SONG

Give me a wild, a virgin place:
Give me a festering, vital hill.

Up-thrusted and humped
The hill is a poem of love
From gods and mists
And ancient heavings.

Twisted and squeezed,
A ball pinched off and rolled about
In the palm of the Lord!

Cracked in the winter of utter contempt
Soaked in the ever-expanding ice-water more fatal than **dynamite**
And more picturesque.

Creased and contorted,
By rivulets hewn:
Crystallized, gravellized
All mashed and all splintered:
Festering.

The hills are lover enough for me:
The pink-cheeked, wrinkled,
Smooth and rolling hills

Are sexual in their embrace:
     I am sucked in.
Like fingers meshed,
Like sleeping lovers
     Rolling, snoring, rousing.
The hills.
Their rhythm
Stretches me taut
And I wander not wonder.

JAMES MARMAR

PATTERNS

Ease and flow of breath,
Minute fingerprints touch and caress.
Warm glowing embers reach out to touch infinity.
Soft cries and hollow melancholiness are cast aside.
Freethink and complete absolutes climb endless staircases,
To the pinpoint of brightness,
At the end of salvation's bridge.

ZERO MINUS POSITIVE

The cool quietness spreads its blanket,
Amid the naked towers.
A light that casts no shadows . . .
A day which never begins . . .
Lonely pebbles sit on limitless beaches,
waiting to be thrown . . .
The dust fills the air with smells of human-like existence,
Never quite settling but hung in suspension.
The pseudo-light spreads its glow,
Trying to warm the earth and make life grow again.
The light fails and the cool quietness silently fulfills the
    prophecy of the sages —
"All that is, will never be so . . . "
The muffled day screams its prayers in silence,
And knows they will not be answered.

KAROLE ANNE MASLEY

REDEMPTION

Dusk settled thickly that year.
Particles, countless and chalky,
Grew into layers,
Choking both flower and weed.
Throughout the clouds, yellow met grey;
And the sun was cancelled out.
The world,
Which first had rung with children's voices,
Was now void of all noise.
Silence settled everywhere.
Suffocation cut the final thread.
Air remained,
But with that air, no breath,
For dusk was there, too;
And to breathe was to die.
Action was already dead.
Round his tomb circled the particles.
There was no escape.

And dusk gave way to night,
A vacuum where children wept silently
And smudged their faces
While brushing away dry tears;
Where men with folded hands
Groped but felt nothing;
Where eyes strained, yet had no vision;
Where lips, once trained to pray, emitted no sounds.

Then gradually an echo unfolded in the hollow tomb.
Airless at first, it steadily deepened.
"Forgive us our knowledge —
Forgive us if we understand, yet do not.
Forgive, forgive, forgive . . ."
A tear fell and soothed the burning face.
Soon it gave place to rain,
And through the black liquid
Could be seen hands uplifted, straining.
The rain continued all night
Then guided Morning to the place.

EDWARD P. MAVRAGIS

DOORS

I have worn the leather of many a shoe
Knocking on doors that refused to listen.
Sometimes I could pry them open a few inches,
But an internal latch kept you out, away.
Some doors did not have handles —
I could only look at them.
Some, some were *even* painted!
Shuffling down this corridor,
An open door bewildered me —
No one could live here!
Peeking inside, my hands worried themselves.
Questioning a tap, I saw my name
On the door and walked in.

A YODEL TO HUMANITY

He was black, so I didn't see him —
He was large, and I heard him
Bouncing twice, once denting my number plate,
The second time, my muffler.
I didn't stop because it didn't look human —
It was only a dog; I prayed though.
Excuses sped through my mind until
Approached by the question:
"How did your car get dented?"
"Someone backed into me."
"then why is fur hanging from your number plate?"
(It *was* a dog!)

FLORISTS

Florists pamper, defend, and glorify their children —
Then spread them out for sale
For the price of a plucked dollar, and

His business is secure, as secure as man's quest
To bury himself respectably —
While alive, while dying, when dead.

His children also die, decaying
With the form they were sold to beautify;
But the florist is noble,
He can plant more seeds to fill in·the holes.

125

HOME

I returned Home
To find you
Waiting.
I embraced you,
But your arms
Paralized,
Did not move.
I kissed you, —
I kissed you
But your lips
Died,
Your eyes remained
Open,
Your heart laughed
Silently,
And I died
Exposed.

J. D. McCLATCHY

EAST COKER: 6 SEPTEMBER 1966

We walked to East Coker from Yeovil,
A short walk, shorter still for the
September summer's morning, warm
And anxious for autumn. White
Doves, fan-tailed on tall pines, waited
Quietly by the vicarage gate, which
Some Gothic spider had traced with
Delicate pride. The sunlight, which
Somewhere the sea was bearing to
Destruction on the rocks, lay gently
On the quivering choir, to warm
A sparrow's winter flight through
Its lighted hall . . .

Beyond the gravel aisle, the church —
Set timidly in the shade, grateful
For an oak at its age — where Andrew
Eliott was baptized in 1627,
Without knowing he was to come
To the New World, without knowing
His later son, who would have
Puzzled him with newknowing the world.

126

And only a clerk and poet.
For East Coker is the breeder of men.
William Dampier's bronzed sea-deeds:
Buccaneer, Explorer, Hydrographer, and
Sometime Captain of the Ship Roebuck in
The Royal Navy of King William the Third.
Even Lady Elizabeth Courtenay
Stands proud with her distinction,
Though time has taken the face from her
Stone. Strong too in their faith:
Feare thou the Lord, and the King
And meddle not with them that are
Given to change. Strong too in
Doubt: old men waiting for
Signs, weaving the dry wind . . .

Among Maudslays and Bullocks,
Beneath the golden-rod and dusty
Light, in a belief more silent
Than death, a poem reminds:

"in my beginning is my end"
Of Your Charity
Pray For The Repose
of the Soul of
Thomas Stearns Eliot
Poet
26 September 1888 — 4 January 1965
"in my end is my beginning"

In your end is my beginning.
In my end is your beginning.
In your end is my end.
In my end . . .

MATTHEW IRVIN McCLINTOCK

MAKE NO WAVES

somewhere in yesterday's wealth
we survived the justice of The Great Society
cathedrals flickered wept wet
reflected passions ultraviolet down stream

movement without motion
vitiated eddies whitecapped in silence
lapped at the mud banks of our idealism

127

tomorrow that same stinking flow
bright for the moth of our phthisic ethic
shall erode more Sunday sermons that move nothing

make no waves hallowed disciplined direction
just mud pies

COB WEB AND THE BARTON SPRINGS
SATURDAY AFTERNOON ARMAGEDDON

to the left of the cotton candy —beyond the dropped fudgecicle flies
no — on the other side beneath the ink blot of the sycamore
see that little boy who's afraid of his fat
jack sprat tide pool ripples of a new generation
annihilation . . .
can he hear us
swimming in his T shirt pup tent trunks
embarrassed tender loin
profound pyramid kiddy looking lurking licking the grotto bottom
everything over his head but
Uncle Wiggily and clark bars
just like his father

NEGOTIATION

I watched you slip from the human fold
Across the concrete stain and prophylactic
Culture inane . . .
I studied you . . . Rhythm Grey . . .
M.olten and pulsating as the sand confirmed

your intrusion . . .
I loved you
While dusk came bleeding through the heavens
to hallow your Solitary frame
Upon its inundated flesh . . .
Solitary . . .
A cosmic ward upon a silent aching beach
Each enervated by the wane tide
fingers of our sire.

128

JOHN McKINNEY

POEM

"C'mon people now, smile on your brother,
Everybody get together, try to love one
another right now."

Chet Powers

the american soldier setting fire to the long
low row of squat thatched roofed shacks faint
puffs of acrid brown smoke stream out the window
then one flame bursting as it crumbles to the

ground . . . the viet cong squad slipping out of the
bamboo rushes quietly rounding up the entire village
screaming children old women twisting their gnarled
dirty hands in anguish a family terrified as the
sword slices smoothly through their father's

neck . . . the small solemn pig-tailed negro child
dressed in clean white cotton jumper skipping
down the street oblivious to the helmeted
guardsmen's flashing bayonets and the hard stares
of the crowd whose red faces scream nigger while
the little girl stops then runs up the school steps

crying . . . the secluded bench under the faint glow
of the central park light an old drunk sleeping it
off awakes to a snapping twig from the bush behind
as three young men sweat on their black faces slap
him across the face and as he screams into the night
the long slender stilletto slips into his soft belly

He sent forth a dove from him, to see if
the waters were abated . . . but the dove found
no rest

Genesis 9

JAMES G. McMILLAN

GALEWINDS BECKONING

I care not for dwellings rising so high.
I care not for the smoke of a stagnant sky.
I can feel little for house choked trees,
And for oak doors in need of keys,
For nature's soil supporting concrete,
For geometrical bricks: elaborate, elite.

I love not a people grouped as so many.
I care not for these, not these or any.
I dream of skys floating and blue,
Of dewy grass with sweet greenish hue,
Of pounding seas thrashing their white,
Galewinds strongly showing their might,
Of whistling birds on whispering trees.
No need of doors here, nor strongly made keys.

SO THIS IS LOVE!

Night falls heavily.
The small study lamp
            illuminates my whispering radio.
Sleeping are the trees
            and tired the breeze that blows no more.
Where's the sun that hid so long ago?
Please wake up!
I feel like talking. Like,
                    Like loving, And
And, Oh, yes. Surely you are sleepless too.

A POEM. A YEARNING.

The rain.
The utter Darkness of night
   confining me to this room.
And those sleeping
   in the other dark chambers.
Oh! While my body aches
   with each passing hour
my heart aches for the taste of soil —
The depth of the Orient,
Salt of a white-capped sea,
The brass of the Slavic
And artistry of Europe,
A savor of Dublin's clover
                    soothing harp,
Scotland's bonnie lassie,
Times Square,
A gong from England's Ancient.
But the rain.
The utter Darkness of night
   confining me to this room.
And those sleeping

130

in the other dark chambers.
A few pages from a treasured old volume,
A willing heart and wandering mind.
A page here, and the next.
A wearied heart.
Some quiet sleep.

MOODS

Moods,
        too schizophrenic
they change a day
                within a day,
        making you persons
and person,
    saying black
            no blue
            now black again
    and back to blue,
    changing,
        ever swirling
        downupward.

TOMMY MEW

ENTRY SUMMER 1965

in the sun i could feel the colour of
autumn floating on the wind soundless
lifting time out of the barn of reality
putting faces on the half moon in the
day sky
            charging down the summer pushing
            august into autumn tainting the
            very air with dreams i could feel
            your eyes plucking past ecstasies
            out of my unquiet heart wrenching
            lust rainbows from my mouth
, softly against my face the scent of
your perfumed hair lay heavy like nectar
            i fabricated love dreams of you
            as summer swept the ochre earth
            like a great silent sea (E)

131

ENTRY 6/30/66

i, in the shadow bent
hills of an early time
the sucked wind wheeling
the trees low
outlined against the pink sky
and the dark green
humping up the air
bellowing the lustre of
our love,
here, in a soft place

while the winding water
waits for fall
we enjoy the subtle scent
of summer
lost in a sacred hollow
dipping daisies from
a full hill field
wild roses,
one in your black hair,

the invite of a willow
while clouds fall into each other
making june full of surprise
gauged the girl
scurried here to fro
absorbed in a new marriage
while a
brown horse idlely
swished time on with each
flick of his tail
chewing a hilled greenfield

the creek running on and on
and i in faded blue jeans
testing myself
by blowing dreams into the
dusk light like ba-lloons,
colour, and full
of hope and success

sloeful litany of the swept hills;
cattail

ONE MORE POEM FOR REMEMBERING

despaired by a splendid sky
erupted in time spewing stars
and a full hanging moon
carefully upon the shadowed
sections of my spelled soul.
i, in a ghostly air, gauged and
garlanded with the fine greenery
of summer swept by
unseasonable rain, soaking the sucked
earth and shouting
a love deep as sky thundering
across the uncertain earth,
flowers swept by the window
of wind.
swayed by the appropriate breeze
of brutal memory
draining the caked land
filling each hollow with perfumed
scents of the chattel mind,

the old eyes of i, in a caught time
whispering the content of your
special look
hearing of you
in a far land,
    in a sweet separate space
hearing of you

as i, in a web of wonder
cast the fallow sky
tilled by cumulus clouds
sprinkled with sex,

i,
    july spent, wished the wild
wind, wrecking honor, won
and
wrested from you in a
secret hallway.
with dark doors leading
to nowhere.

i spent your eyes today
in a subtle effort to bring it all back
    despaired, i

WILLIAM A. MEYER, JR.

VICTOR

To gaze on ocean eyes
Infinity this glance moves.
Unexpectant glow strokes the whole of me
Awareness of this wish lends hands.
Tranquil light . . . offer recognition.
Slow breath . . . breathe time.
Patient thought never eludes
Peace . . . quiets motion.

GARY EDWIN MILLER

TRAIN SUNDAY

On tressle wood
before midmorning is
a wan boy
skimming flatstones on channel ice
in winter
his tattered patcharm spinning the sad
lone birds of hard earth humming
toward the frozen shore
this side of town's
end
the rock dead
sound losing breath
against the pounding moan
of iron on iron that roars in
the year of the hammer and the road
way dance of pretending children that turns
its rosy face in order to be fed by the mystery
trident of a church pure state while
flatstones clatter by the steeple
deep chants that are hymn
bringing the home warm
sun from behind an
altar
but it's winter
and cloud cold flinging
handfuls of flatstones deaf
in rail thunder through
the rag boy's silent
song soars of a
David slinging.

THE LIMBUS TREE

anachronous
am i
as i stand young at time,
brainless in the phase dichotomy of
the minute but celestial spheres that compose this eyeshell form.
The dual disc sun of my other body converges every shape
the sense into one which forgets what it was
but remembers that it is being free
except for itself.
Here
i stand young at time,
knowing that a limekiln burns shells to lime,
yet i listen for the bells in the moon, and exalt
in the magic prism of the limbus tree
as it imitates the radiance
on the other side.
and
i am ofttimes a fool
anachronous to the last ascent
of that highest brilliance
into the birth of
the humblest
things.

THE GOOD SULTAN MIDGE

The
good sultan midge
juggled
his warhump
in a bent bone cage
the three ring dwarf
calamity
of his day clown
act
laughing its
numb chalk mask
as the catharsis
of the tragic
hooked juggler
arced
high uprain
from the lyric
bass tones

135

```
                    underbridge
          His
              staccato rhythm
                            climb
              more and more
                  halting
                          as the asylum
              of something that waited
                      at the looping crest
              breathed  jump
                    and he did it
              thinking of
                          freedom
              from the sad
                          circus part
              he left in the water.
```

GERALD MILLER

FACTORY

Raised eyes following the line skyward
View the throbbing creation.
Blackened walls attest to
The banging of progress.

Enter the well-trod gates
And hear the hum of the factory.

The gray morning skies
Are the heralds crying a new day.
Slowly, one by one, the factory awakes
Stretching and yawning as does a beautiful woman at dawn.

Senses come into being
And the heart beats faster.
Turning and looking upon the vast streets,
She blares out her defiance of the void.

Blast furnaces fume
And boil and red steel blood
That is formed God-like into creation.

Cams spin
And stamping machines sing
Their virile song of ecstasy.

The little wheel turns,
And the big wheel grinds
Out the hammering harmony of living.

SONNET

Bob-white whistles song's sweetness under yellowed tree
Above the flattened plains of burnished gold sea.
Delicate beetles click to beat
During the heavy felt summer heat.

Fat hours, the dewy mist early days
Of mid-morning, sunlit silenced haze.
Wind sprite turn farmer's path
Into whirling dervishes of whimsical wind's wrath.

And slowly the willow
Bends its hanging branches yellow
With age; time trusted, sun shone,
Growing upon a grass banked hill, yet alone.

Life is like that age-drooped tree,
To be alone, but to understand summer beautifully.

MOURNER'S KADDISH

Damn it. A man ain't supposed to cry.
                    Let . . .
Yell into the pale void
of birth control pills.
                    his . . .
Tears upon a lonely, frozen planct
where no one hears the hungry kids.
                    great . . .
Bulged eyes scream in gray mist
and can't close and pray.
                    Name . . .
Knees bent in a graveyard
that is the gasp in muffled whimpering.
                    be . . .
I can't say it together, Lord.
I've seen too many double amputees
begging in the street.
                    blessed . . .
I've seen the bent cleaning women
pulling at their black rags.
                    for ever . . .
I've seen too many photographs
of happy faces now contorted
in silent anguish.

137

and . . .
I've seen too many old men
sitting on cracked benches
drawing in lonely pipe smoke,
              to all . . .
I've seen too many people curse
and fling their beer at —
              They don't know what . . .
                   eternity.

ERIN MONRONEY

THE DANCE AND THE DINNER AFTERWARDS

Blue arms flicker-fickle
through hot polka dot stars
              and
spotted spoons drop carelessly
into tank green sulphur pools
with other skeletons at the bottom.

BULLFIGHT

Animal —
nice
paschal
sacrifice
—funny
genuine
runny
sanguine
red,
thrills
spread
spills
part
art.

NOW OR COMING

With the sun shone on by a blue sky
—a pistachio mint
that just had an earthquake
existing a mechanic's mess,
but the gulls sit stupid,
unflying,
grey and not yet gone.

138

DOROTHY BUTLER MORELAND

POEM

Let the churning, muddy stream of life pass quickly by me;
cover my eyes, make me blind
then I cannot see,

  all the cruelness and foul deeds puked forth from the very bowels of
  this creature called man;
   civilized he professes to be, yet, he carries an aura of evil,
    as the snake slithering through water, squirming across land.

Let me close my ears tightly, so that I may not hear
the sound of ignorance, the sound of fear
 the sound of mass hatred cracking against the very core of my existence;
  the sound of crumbling will-power as I am slowly stripped of my last
  shred of resistance.

Let me encompass myself completely within the protective womb of
''I don't give a damn,'' then, I will not feel
 the hot breath of viciousness steaming profusely from the acid vat
 deep in the heart of man — man, the ideal.

SWEET DEATH

Let me not awake tomorrow morning for the next twenty years,
 let the peaceful slumber of death soothe the savage fingers,
that not unlike jagged thorns, tear and rip away at my soul
 unleashing a flood of useless tears.

Oh, beautiful sleep of the dead, come, come to me tonight, come
 rest yourself upon the head of my bed,
carefully, very carefully, take the hem of your soft hooded robe
and wipe away the smear of color left by a heart of stone that
 crumbled and bled.

Touch my forehead ever so lightly so that I may reach up and
know that you are there,
 waiting, waiting to bring relief to this poor lost soul who
thought that she couldn't care.

I cannot, I will not awake to another dawn to feel the heartache,
 wanting, and loneliness slowly creep in,
I will not face the dreadful pain of wishing hopelessly for the
continuance of something wonderful that should never have been.

Yes, peaceful death, I will wait for you to come, to take me away,
 to let me rest forever free from pain, pain that I cannot bear
even for one more day.

139

JAMES A. MULLER

THE LATE SHOW

A bluish gleam convulses a man in a chair,
Or rather what he makes of it
Releases the energy of tension caused
By the strictures of man's limits.
Death, illness, and even the pain
Of too-confining shoes bind one
Like a compressed spring which
Vibrates vigorously when freed.

But deep down laughter never convulses.
Down deep *unus mundi* knows
Man has no limits.
He springs the universe.

bluehazelaughingman

ANN C. MURPHY

Sounds of wood cry out at the night dawns
And the coroner celebrates this time with candles and a cake
A striped coyote rises to the hooting moon
Who with patient hands conjures up the dead
But they will not listen to a beacon light
In vain the trapped coyote summons them
The coroner means to eat his cake alone
For the company he lacks has canine candles
Sounds of wrinkled wire curse the dusk
Now the coffin-boats are caulked and tarred with jam
Our bonnets frantic and confining
Make us hesitate and cough before the fallen day

I sit and read to
The music of the hair dryer
Wire higher fire
It's magnetic
Copesetic
As it whines and dries
Brings tears to my eyes
Heats the pins til they sear
The tender flesh behind my ear
All the oils of my scalp
Shrivel up flake out
Wire coils curly coils
Curlicues for my muse.

140

MICHAEL H. MURRAY

RELEVANCE

When once the drone of Mr. Osgood's rasping,
Reaching, barely short of preaching, literary
Analytical voice . . . approached (sixteen)
Indolently fragmented, inattentive me . . .
"Tran-zhents," he seemed to lisp, or sought the long
Evaporated ice of fouled-up Frank,
Then pivoted to Frosty gold where dawn
Sank down to (?) leafmeal or the like, and on
To Alfred J. and burnt-end stubs unrolled.
"To the greatest" — signaling a page (Oh!
Fumble, shift) — "speaker on this theme (Plain Bill),"
Then: ember fires, sere leaves, brown birds in choirs . . .
Oh damn! gone bad . . . my desk-hid fingers sunk
In once gold orange rind gone squish-gray-green.

THOMAS MYROUP

OBSERVATION DECK

Now as street lights scratch the night
and headlights squirm amid downtown buildings,
I look through the glass,
smudged by the fingers and noses of children,
by the tobacco breath of adults,
the glass of the observation deck.
I look down on tiny man (sick with seed and Sanka,
trying to suck the nipples of the stars)
and hope that from fifty stories of relative space,
I too am being observed.
All the strutting babblers have left;
alone above the city I stand
and by the little lightning flash of my cigarette lighter
read the law:
"Observation Deck Closes at One A.M."

THE MIST

The mist lies upon the valley,
like a lover on the beloved,
gently, tenderly, weightlessly
at night: star still, cloud-clear, moon mounts.

141

A tree tarries on a hillside,
bowing in private prayer.
Shadows sleep near some houses
in the nodding night air.

The mist rises from the valley,
like a lover from the beloved,
gently, tenderly, weightlessly
at dawn: silky sun — cloud rimmed — drones.

ROBERT NECKER

LATE AUTUMN

The wind weaves through
puddles of rain-ripped red
leaves and autumn flows in the
wind's veins and the night
runs cold as a witch-wooed apple.

But the moon sits still
as a schoolroom clock
whose ticktock full
and final is, as: a cat's
wink, a monk's Amen.
Then Time tiptoes.

And we dream, the wind brings
sounds, leaves break. We dream
of windows and snow outside — one
dream I died.
And woke snowbound.

SUSAN NEUBERGER

LET'S HEAR IT FROM THE FOLKS UNDER THE THEATRE

The snows of bygone years are mixed with bones of bygone men
Somewhere underneath top ground they lie
All in earth now melted and diffused.
The lofty thoughts of poets seep in streams of brackish slime
The silenced wants of women drip to pools of mold
Body's beauty falls to maggots
Holy cravings left to rot in peace.
To think of passions, plans, plots and people carving the canals of Hell
Underneath my house! Cankered corpses oozing into tunnels
Six feet from the whiteness of my sheets!

Each day I walk upon their heads, and arms, and death-clutched hands
Dance inches over vacant eyes and bits of brain
Continue to perform the life routine for underground voyeurs —
Not because I fear, or laugh at death,
I live, and therefore am too late to dread the outcome —
I do it to amuse the bones and staring eyes,
Who have no other jokes to tell
I dance so they can smile
And feel relief at their escape,
The greatest joke of all.

Someday, when I die and carve my own dark rivers,
You must dance for me.
Then I, in my dark warm and quiet rest
Will laugh at you in your stiff white and living bed.

MASS PRODUCTION

Why, why are all the people silent?
All I see are rows of eyes
Glassy mirrors, mute reflectors
Mouths repeating well-learned phrases
Hearts attacking right on signal
Faces moving in assembly
Minds in stick-men, each a puppet
Each a mirror, all in rows
Foppish faces no one knows.

Why, why are all the people silent?
All I see are rows of colors
Arms extended, lashed together
(Loving if the light says *"GO"*
Hating if the sign says *"NO"*)
Eyes evading other lenses
Mouths evading different answers
Vacant smiles, blinding blackness
Empty giggles, blatant grins
One million straw-men all in rows
Softly praying someone knows.

Why, why are all the people silent?
All I see are rows of flannel
Legs beat time to faces' death
Mirrors splinter, smiles broken
Mouths that drool with specious rhyme
Thin legs marching, marching, marching.
Faithful faces, men in rows
Off the cliff so nothing shows.

143

MERCY

When everything else was spent —
Need, love, energy, concern —
And all we could do was lie
Quietly, only breathing, only
Remembering each other,
But still touching, so as not to be lost
In vacant abstract memory
(Did you notice it then?
That my one finger rested on your hand,
After, I being afraid
To touch you more. Silly)
But when everything else had gone —
Wanting, giving, taking more —
When we were quiet for a while
(And of course a little breeze came in the window,
The sun shone but not brightly, a little veiled,
And not even a stray clock went off, of course not)
We were very, very still.
But then I, feeling like
A taken woman of the movies,
Blissfully exhausted,
I turned to you
And kissed you.
Which of course, in view of past events,
Was really nothing, but it was special
Because, well, of its sweetness.
A kiss hung there,
In the little breeze
And the veiled sun, hung there
In the imagined silence, hung
For a long-short minute, and
Everything was suspended, until
A stray clock went off and the sun came out.

RICHARD NEWHAUSER

POEM

So you've kissed her and held her hand,
    that girl with bright eyes looking at you —
        through you —
            to the people
    and modes of reality out there.

144

Yes, you love her
>   short hair
>   firm flesh
>   warm emotional laugh
>   too-cute nose
>   childlike release from drudgery.

But don't think for a moment
>   you pompous ass
>   that she belongs to you,
>   for she is a
>   child of the world
>   and when it calls,
>   like the flight of the birds,
>   she will go.

MOLLY OSBORNE

TWO

An electric spark
Softly forming a tender wire
Lengthening and expanding
Beautiful in its simplicity
With exquisite depth.

Twining and intertwining
Reaching out gently
And suddenly met.

The shrinking back
The weaving within
The delicate probing
Of another.

The clash of the meeting
The triumph and despair
In an effort to combine
The thunder and lightning
To find a meaning
Between two.

And gradually
A soft awakening
A slow joining
Of the scintillating wires.

145

LOVE

A soul blooms under Love
Gentle star-lit paths
Expand outward as rippling water
Pours through channels
Of orange Paradise.
A soul

Runs down rich green arcades
Rivulets sprinkling joy
As fine and plentiful
As dust to the wind —

A. APPLETON PACKARD

FROM MY WINDOW

Wake to this dawn,
Curtains withdrawn,
Over the lawn
Upspringing day.

Lilac leaves hold
Dewdrops of gold
— Treasure untold —
Poetry's play.

Give terror truce,
Dream-fears unloose,
Let that blue spruce
Point to release.

Sing in the sun,
Daylight begun,
Darkness outrun;
Trumpets sing peace!

GREGORY KNIGHT PAGE

FIVE POEMS

hollow eyes stare into emptiness,
the blackness overwhelming.
out of the pitch sea
flies a big black bird.

146

talons raking the tender flesh
of the senseless multitudes
who have gathered to watch
the slaughter of others.
hollow eyes, picked clean
by the ravenous bird
feasting on the folly of man,
stare blankly
from the smiling skulls.

he rose alone,
faltering in the night
and winged toward the moon
and stars.
the horologe measured the meter
of his incessant wings
hardly heard against the stillness
of the night.
in the vast void
between earth, moon, and stars
he made his own life's journey,
alone . . .
but there were others journeying,
some near,
some obscure in the distance.
with a precious few
he chased stars
until after some sweet interlude
he was again
alone . . .
and from the phantasmagoria of life
he sought another star,
promising warmth;
and his insatiable search for warmth
carried him on
and on
and . . .
as his journey waned
and the horologe beat faster,
his wings beat slower
and he reminisced about his journey.
he rose alone,
faltering in the night
and before the distant dawn broke
he was gone.

147

sitting, watching
ashes dropping,
boring words
fill the minutes.
slowly, slowly
time passes
as the ashes fall.
when the bell
next calls an end
to the boring words
we will stop
our sitting, watching
but the ashes will
cover
the floor.

the moon is risen, finally full,
enthroned in her solitary setting.
alone in the unfathomed darkness
she sits,
lugubriously lamenting life.
scrutinizing life from afar,
then near,
orbiting the fringe of life
not satisfied with prosaic ways.
precluding darkness where she glides
in her search;
pallid silver'd beams emitted,
garnered by the encircling multitude
that crowds the celestial beauty.
for those who gaze
upon the mystic journey,
awe struck,
the night is illuminated
by the portentous light.
the moon is risen,
finally full —
    what of life will its waning years construe,
    how shall the requiem read —

lines parallel,
obtuse, and right
before my eyes
with broad planes
transversely cut
and flattened
parallelograms
sit.
numbers, formulas,
square rooted equasions
all in nonesense
my mind attack.
but finally all knowledge
is put in proper place
by one broad erasure sweep.

JOHN STEPHEN PAUL

THREE POEMS

Among the vast and clear,
far and near,
amidst that which flows,
that which grows,
above all,
and beyond all
we stand and tremble at what we know
we stand and shout as the winds blow
the cold
the dim
and beyond us: there are smiles.

My life is the jungle
my days are the night
Don't touch me baby
I don't want to fight
Just kiss my tongue
and I'll let you pass
and please give my boss a piece of your ass.
When they pile it on I'll kick it off
and when I show them that I got the stuff
I'll console the lampost and spit up my cuff
and chop down the trees
and turn on the lights
and piss on the lawn and make everything right.

And yet to exist is to smile
And yet to exist is to walk on the water
of memories past,
of things you have done,
of darkened days.

And yet to exist
to exist in the billowing curls of my love's flesh
the watery smile in that darkened eye.

And yet to exist and kiss in the icy wind
those thoughts of the past,
on the rocks,
on the shore,
with the water over my feet.

And to exist in that world which never exists,
where the wealth abounds
And the sun's warmth cleans the soul of the lost traveler.

    To ride your elephant in the triumphal march through
cheering crowds
And love all,
Have all
Then awake to the chill of one more coffee cup's last sip.

GARETH S. PENN

EASTER

Poinsettias pranced in the winds of the springtime,
brilliant red blossoms blown wet in the rain
vernally swirled in a whirligig swingtime:
millions of flowers were dancing again —

Orchards were yellow, the mustard in masses
trooping to westward and dancing in hand;
and up in the foothills and high granite passes
lupen most purply leaped overland.

Brazen the kelpswells in waves rolling lazily —
wasn't the seaweed washed up in the coves?
Retiringly, modestly, dogwoodly, daisily,
cousins embodiced in dark redwood groves . . .

Poinsettias flying like sparks from a fire:
how they sprang and cavorted, contorted and whirled
to the melody played by the wind on his lyre —
now the flowers are dancing all over the world!

150

JOHN PERDOMO

THOUGHTS OF YESTERDAY

How funny to think / magic vibrations /
Of love touch kiss / disappeared from southern
Bound winds . . .
Passed is a time / place . . .
Which would / would not have existed . . .
Nor are few stains of meaningful days /
Hours / seconds forgotten . . .
Paper airplanes floating / bombarding my mind
With memories . . .
Remembering / loving a dream / dreams . . .
A warm / smiling being / understanding/
Not understanding / loving / not loving . . .
The sun warms my body / as I sit under a tree /
In a park / in myself /
       Remembering ????

NOAH PESSAH

TOO ATTRACTIVE

On my tiny, modern table,
covered with a white artfully
designed linen spread,
ostentatiously features
a basket full of red,
fresh, juicy apples.
A sparklingly sharp, brutal
knife sticks among them.
Both get close together.
Inevitably, the knife seems
to get excited.
Its ferocious appetite
sharpens, threatening
to annihilate the edible
fruit one by one.
In candor:
The crisp, fleshy, red,
round apples are too
attractive to be left
untouched . . .

151

JOHN PETERS

LONELINESS

wilting leaves
dying flowers
bleached white bones
falling towers
burning rocks
an aged tree
leaveless branch
and only me

DAVID W. PINCHBECK

A MIGHTY FORTRESS SIGNIFYING NOTHING

Cabinets stand straight and tall,
Full of papers written in hieroglyphics,
Stacked on top with more papers.

Maps roll off the top and lie sprawled
Upon the linoleum floor.
The linoleum is laid in neat squares
Fraught with unintelligible patterns.

Another cabinet holds cards;
Index keys to the hieroglyphs
Which are in turn symbols of something else.
Where does it end?

Typewriters click and voices drone.
Bald heads and cold metal abound.
Ulcers vie with spastic diaphragms for miserable lives
    already dead.

A jumble of papers, clips, staplers, pencils, and figures
Swim on my desk and through my brain.
The smell of strong cigars assails my nose.

Garbage pails flow over with remnants of the hieroglyphs
No longer useful.
Pigeon holes line the walls for ink and leads and blotters.
Pigeon holes line the halls for old and bald and hopeless.

Maps on the walls drawn by spiders are webs for idiots.

From my air conditioned bastille of bedlam I can see little
For the windows are dirty and my glasses need strengthening.

Outside the sun is shining.

152

REMEMBER . . . I PASSED THIS WAY

Carve my name on the tree of time,
Write my name in the sand.
Say my name on the winds of time,
And send my name on the wings of time,
And never forget, never forget,
I was.

SANFORD PINSKER

THE CELEBRATION

With one arm dragging down uselessly
We wheeled around my hardwood floor —
Furniture flying; your hair in my face
And the pictures clinging, like plants, to the wall.
With books set aside and glasses askew
You taught me all there was of turn
Until I was soft and the self crept out
To mingle with what you were open.
My motion circled in its measured movement
(Like some old steamer out to sea again)
Plunging all my feeling mast
Into the webby wetness of your mound.
Coming to port is journey's end —
I celebrate myself in you.

THEME #1

O menders of splices and fixers of fragments,
Autumn is icumen in; more cuckoos for your chorus.
I suited up for the new fall season —
Patched, pressed and starched to the neck;
An academic player ready for the game again.
My Byronic feet kept limping along
(The meter slows these days to a stop.)
And I needed a jockstrap to protect my ear.
Creeping around the edges of academe,
I looked at beauties with a bloodshot eye.
But that was before the resounding theme
Came crashing back in a thousand fragments.
Things have started to slide since then;
I'm losing my grip on the slopes of Parnassus.
Even my ink is running short
(I can feel the red stuff flowing out)
As I cement the sins of their last summer
With words that dance a dying tune
And fall back in the mold once more.

153

J. J. POPSON

HERE IT IS

Here it is,
The dispelling of an illusion:
Was the king fated to fall?
Richard screamed and lost his grip;
Why not I — all for eternity,
Simply die the simple death.
The last drop of crimson blood
Will fall upon the breast of time
And dry as slowly as the eye does close.
Earth, merry, happy, cooling earth!
Surround the limbs that unite with roots
Of ancient ash trees
In splendor and longing
For the dim light of ending.
It has been a weary day,
Drained of simple love and touching hands;
Chains have bound a golden wheel
That threatened rolling to the sea.
None can feel the tear-stained face,
For it has dropped into its hiding place.
The passion now is hard to find
And is not a fevered hope sublime;
Easy mind and body melting
Have no home in cold, grey skies,
But looking there instills a cry
That lies deep in the soul of some
Lost minister of the "Gospel of Fun".
No thanks! I will tear apart waves
And cast them into hearts that are cracked —
Maybe a shock will loosen what is masked
And drown that image of something that saves.

S, COLD DAY, COLD NIGHT,
FAINT FLICKER OF DISTANT LIGHT

I have a scream coming for you
Out of darkness
A plea
The desire is to grow
With a slow beauty
To never know all about
The sparkles that glance from your eyes

154

To the shadows.
The forest hides its growing beauty
The sun breaks in
On some secret life
But much never is illumined
A tear can be touched
And dry.
I can taste a breath
Wash my mind with a word
Struggle to see a soul
Sense joy
Feel warmth
Swell full . . . for a time
Then trip, lonely, toward a cold, rain-battered lamp
Set too far for weary feet.
The walking with splashes
The crashing of raindrops
Upon soft face
And hard pavement
(Nowhere is it all soft)
And then I laugh
Begin to run
Thundering along in time
To my own breathing
Slipping and spinning to a step.
A scream for you —
Or part

DOROTHY J. POLLOCK

THE YUCCA

For me a desert flower, creamy clustered;
    A lilly, yet not of the purest white.
Queen of the wilderness, chaste, proud, unflustered
    There among barren rocks bathed in sunlight.

An alien to the sea, the foamy spray,
    Like the wave's cap, caught on a stately stalk,
Rises above thirsty sands to gently sway
    In the breeze, far from the traveler's walk.

A complement to the desert's sunny sweep,
    Castled in sharp-tipped dagger leaves, wild-wise,
The Yucca reigns, and silently I must weep
    To leave this kingdom lest fantasy dies.

155

SONORA DROUGHT

Ruthless, unmoving, the great sun hangs still,
Cauterizing the already parched earth.
Prolonged noon, day's hated hour, ever will
Be unwelcomed here, no visible worth.

The evil sun at day's peak marks the time
For needed rest, sustenance, time to think,
Yet in this rainless, God-forsaken clime
One hates the noon when there's no food or drink.

THE CHIRICAHUAS

Flaming, reluctant sunset lingers there
Over the Chiricahuas where no sound
Echoes through the grotesque goblin rocks where
Guns once blazed, speeding arrows fell to ground,
For the dark of night brings back warriors old,
Shadowy ghost-shapes, spirits of unrest,
To dance in bone-dust of unburied bold,
Wailing the blotched fame of a dying West.

JOHN A. POULOS

Your spirit surrounded me.
Your desires, my duties to fulfil.
Your quaking body, my satisfaction in motion.
Your final breath of pleasure, my resurrection.

My hands still smell of you.
My heart still grieves your departure.
My ears still probe the dark for your whisper.
My chapped body craves the shelter of your smooth warmth.
My lips still sore from your ardor,
Express only appreciation of your person.

My memories of past pleasures
Are wiped clean in the wake of our experience.

156

NEXT WEDNESDAY #1

Silently and sadly writing,
Not knowing really what I want to say.

How to choose and put together
A thousand thoughts running rampant.

Love? Yes, I know of it.
What more should I say?

I wallow in it when I can,
And then wonder if that's bad.

To hear my name on the lips of sweet sincerity herself.
To feel the pulsing warmth of a grateful breast.

Ah, but Love is more than this you say.
I might agree, but there is little more I know to say.

I can only stammer a few inadequacies,
Compounding my confusion and diluting the essence
      of that which I am honoring.

Salty. Not really.
Sweet. No, more than that.

More than a fragrance.
More an essence.
An experience.
A time of being.
A memory.
A way of remembering.

Hers more memorable than the others.
Some acid, repulsive;
Others bearable.
Hers enjoyable in itself.
I longed for it,
I pleasured in it.

Neither stagnant nor sour,
Nor purely honey or rose.
Completely unique.
Completely delightful.
Completely Hers;
      Sometimes gratefully mine.

157

LARRY PRICE

A HIGH PLACE

Hohenhasslach.
we lived in that village for a year.
the name, we learned,
meant
a High Place for Rabbits.

never too friendly,
always aloof,
the farmers went by cart and tractor to the fields and vineyards
to till and reap as taught by foregoing centuries.

we were a novelty
to be stared at, talked about.
a lone american couple
with child
who lived spartan-like in this wayside hamlet,
where there was neither place nor time for such as we.

they did not understand
why we wandered dreamy-eyed through their fields and forests,
why i wore tight pants and sneakers and was pale from lack of sun,
why our mouths were hushed by the sight of their antelope-deer,
why, when conversation abounded, we were silent and sad.

they could not understand
why we had stopped crying for John Kennedy when they had not,
why we felt compelled to live in a place where we had no place,
why we put our army in vietnam (we were American no matter how we felt).

and it irked us that we knew little more than they;
only that somehow an ambiguous america had driven us there.

when at last we left the village,
the houses and streets were silent,
faces watched from windows
passively.
in a year our souls had been nurtured by their coolness.
the cold blue eyes saw through our shams, till, in the final days,
even we saw the dismal shadows we cast.

our departure was quick and unadorned with sentiment,
for what we left behind would never be missed.
the train shuttled away quickly, village and town passing,
until the last vision of the place was gone.
the vision of a place
which was indeed
a High Place for Rabbits.

MARY E. PSARRAS

THREE POEMS

The wind blew the leaves
And rose the words in the night
And I followed
But where they went was difficult to learn
through the spears of grass cathedrals of archaic **belief**
that pointed against the sky
blue and lighted by the moon.
Full it was
But cast no light on lost symbols
of meanings yet to be found.
The dumbed body bled in the maze of forgotten **faith**
in the nothingness that separated it
from the white light.
When the wind blows
and the pages turn, again
will the night conceal the words,
the spears of fate
by which we bleed?
What wind is this,
what torment of the night —
that nothingness that separates, conceals —
in which we live?
Where is the sun, that greater light
to sear the flesh, reflect the earth
reveal the grass, the mountains and beyond?
Will it rise? Will it rise
                    tomorrow
                        will it rise?

The wilderness of time
is a bell that echoes for the dead
And what abstractions do we find
to comfort our lost
living eternally
        in light of time
        we do not see, we do not read
        in days of our past
        the beginning and end
        the prism of time
        with colors therein.

159

The moth to the incandescent globe
clings — extinguishes life
without remembrances it never had.
But man in solitude hangs
Sways in the shade of the dead
With his memories he never knew,
his lost
and the winding road of cypress trees pointed
and shaped by the form of color and space
roots clinging to the soil
stemming to the light
living in the seed.
The man weeps
And the intervals resound.

The city streets,
Abstract areas of familiarity
without human touch or smell
in the light of the sun
fill the eye with shapes,
the ear with distant sounds,
and rest the mind.
The daylight is shade for the reflections
that beg the moon,
the white light that reveals
the passivity of ourselves
suspended in the light of the sun.
The pain loosens
in the extension of weariness —
loses a little its despair
allowing the mind to wander at will.
The city streets,
abstract areas of familiarity
without human touch or smell
and our abstract selves
find abstract harmony.

VINCENT PAUL QUINN

TORCH — 1960

What's left of life is little.
Perhaps these shards — dust devils
On a sunny road, a noon-warm grove

Of pine, the almost soundless ripple
Of the shore-met sea. That's all,
But they're mine.

When that wondrous you was gone,
These remained beyond the empty door
Through which you went,
And they are in my eyes and ears,
When round the tight-fleshed cage of me
Other arms are bent.

You have marked the deathless things
And though I have no portrait, note,
Or souvenir, when in the air of summer
I see oleanders blowing white and pink,
My hands fall numb. I cannot think.

Then dumb I stand with questioning.
Is there any happiness beyond this sight,
Or do I dare to wish that all I had before
Will come again exultantly
Through that same door.

GAIL ANGELA RACKLEY

THOUGHT SOFTLY

To trace the secrets
            — of your smile
Through the contemplation of your world

To seek the patterns
            — of your mind
Through the unveiling . . .
                        Of your gentle and kind words

Your touch — excitation —
                        solaced me

To be with you . . .
            beside you in the dark
Though the passing of our hours —   so few

Your eyes have told me many things
— of things unknown to me —
While holding me —
            expressions —

wandering, changing — swiftly hard — soft**en**ing —
Did not escape my own
     Though surely not for me

Your hands
     Yes, your knowing hands — a com**fort**

And oh to make me laugh!

So much more, so very much more
. . . Told in better ways . . . All unsaid

I will think of these often
And miss — In the passing of your decisions —
     Because I care for you.

ON BECOMING 23

So, you wish

   To have

     To laugh

       To feel

         To hold

           To cry

             To love

               To dream

                 Too old.

JEFFERSON RAHILL

RUNNING

Running,
swimming,
jumping,
and being happy and things
drinking
and taking trips
of all sorts and kinds
because the *real* finds
are in the mind.

BUGS AN'

Bugs an'
lizards an'
rats an'
spiders an'
creepies an'
crawlies are
sneaking in
my bedroom window.
It's plain to see
they're after me
for now I fear
my time is here.
Closer and closer
they draw to me.
I close my eyes
afraid to see
their pinchers and feelers
and fangs and stingers
on their fingers,
and as I realize
I'm only dreamin'
their head spokesman
says, "we're only tryin'
to scare ya."

SHADES OF YOUTH MINUS ONE

Mashed potatoes and pot
can be a lot
of fun to stick your
fingers into . . . or so they say

Why do you want my shoe?
It's too big for you,
but I guess you could wear it on your ear . . .
if you're a tiger that is.

If you've got stripes
don't run too fast
especially around the gutter
unless you want to be butter.

And above all else
no matter what he tells
you, don't let go of the balloon
because you never can tell with bees.

163

IT ALL DEPENDS

Push through school
don't be a fool
and mess around
or you'll be found
at the bottom
when the money
is passed around.
Don't waste time
move ahead
be successful
and secure a place
for yourself in
heaven and the
community too.
Go to church
and don't search
for other things
or lurk
in the wings
on the dark side
of society
for the other way
shall be left
to the minds
that are deft
in understanding
the possibilities
of other ways . . .
but it all depends
on what
you believe in.

IT'S LATE

You can't
concentrate
when it's
late
because the
sounds are filling
the air
and you,
with the feeling
that is

pulsating
and perpetual
and flowing
through you.
Mixed up
in the
complete sound
of the music
with the notes
driving you to
express the beat
and get on
your feet
you wonder why
you can't
drop everything
and fly.

EDWARD C. RAMIREZ

A MOMENT OF SILENCE — SPARED TO REFLECT

A moment of silence,
Spared to reflect,
My conscience commands
of my soul to inspect.
Of things I must strive,
Or things which should,
Of things had I time,
I certainly would.
Of good intent,
Things if I could,
These things which derive from my pensive
mood.
A moment of silence,
yes, here to reflect,
Upon all these things I had left to neglect.

SAILS OF LAKE MERRITT

Sails of Lake Merritt are gently blown.
Boats, under urban sky, sail alone.
Hoist up the sail;
Cast off the rope;
Glide with the breeze at an angular slope.

'Round past fowl islands on a tiny sea —
Where swans and geese cool under a tree.
Sails of Lake Merritt are never free,
Embraced by the city, yet, lovely to see.
Bright, little vessels with no place to go
sail along when the breezes blow.
Around and around, the boats sail by —
captured beneath the wide, urban sky.

EGRAM RAMS

THE LEGACY

The meek shall inherit the earth.
What will the inheritance be?
Hills and dales of variegated greens?
Intense azure skies, with fleecy clouds,
Meandering throughout like fuzzy white
Lambs playing a game of "catch me quick?"
Majestic snow-capped mountains
Standing guard over forest and field?
Graceful statuesque trees, standing
Tall and straight as sentinels?
Many-hued birds soaring high above
Their voices lifted in joyous song?
The animals, gentle and friendly?
All men at peace, truly brotherly?
No! When the last will and testament
Is read, you shall inherit napalm
Blackened hills and forests.
Strontium saturated atmosphere.
Crumbled piles of mountains. The birds
Song silent as death. Barbecued
Fauna strewn on the charred
Crust of the earth, side by side
With the festering remains of my brothers.
This is your legacy, bequeathed
To one and all by the aggressors!
Death spreads his cape and the
Shadow encompasses the whole world.
The final and permanent Heir ! ! !

MARTIN A. RANFT

My goats-feet heart hurts
Every promise made to straighten each day's thought.
My feel-foolish temper richens
Time to density of moments never sought nor
Found nor wanted.

She rivals single pains
In inch renewal of my mind to single wish
Uncalled. Or does she pause
To drain and soothe and fill again
My goats-feet heart?

ON PASSING ROOM 209, FOURTH PERIOD

There she perches, in her carriage
Stark upstartled, quizzically leaning upright
To know you. This pert nearness of her self
Which flowers all my mind with sunbursts
Of pure reason for things hidden seen clear
Devours all that's soul and all the heart besides.

How that foreign tongue of self
Declines response to pressure days of living
Molded pasts that telescope our days,
And yet surprises self in self on fire
To just the touch of nearness.

ARLENE R. RASMUSSEN

REALIZATION

The dull light of a 40 watt bulb
dangling precariously on the brink of infinity
by a frayed and blackened wire,
                        its only life line.
The tarnished silver chain dances helplessly
moved and stilled by whims that come and go,
so helpless,
so dependent,
the frugal little sounds it utters;
no character,
no rhythm,

my one noted music box
                tied to the ceiling.
I'm alone,
so deafeningly alone.
Am I that chain, silver and cheap,
filled with false pride in my importance?
My thoughts —
                without me —
                        darkness,
only to discover I was nothing alone,
just a link,
an almost obsolete link
in a chain reaction
                and easily bypassed.
Who told me?
Who turned out my light and ground it
                into the dirt of reality?
Who killed me?
My family, my friends, myself?
What does man live for
                but for his ideals?
Tell me!
What else is there to live for?

SUZANNE RECTOR

FACES

Lying like an eyeglass
is the sea reflecting the sky
and dark forboding clouds,
and the winged lookout
whose shadow
circles, — then leaves.

A thousand faces has the
sea, lying beneath where
none can see.
A tidal wave, gentle waves, and a white
capped storm are waiting
to become.
A thousand faces, — but
none of its own.

168

PETER B. REMLER

WORDS

Poems to write
in days like these
are efforts of the mind.
(Conjuring images for vast fortresses
of ill reason and lies.)
Poems to write
should be for truth
but in these days,
the grey days,
tumbling down stupidly
upon us
poems to write
become the last defense
against defiling words
and foul speeches
that make the world all wrong.
Poems to write
are words of poems
to set the words aright:

1) What grey days loom ahead;
   The fog reveals the dead words
   stillborn on their speaker's lips.
2) Endless, meaningless words
   not to explain our own
   uncomprehending death.
3) Or words packed in cans,
   pre-frozen for export.

The mind conjures many images,
disemboweling its own self
for words it cannot express.
(The word's all wrong.
The meaning's gone.
Unhinge the mind from words.)
Eyes say things.
And the mind's eye
sees the fog of frozen, boneless words.

ENID HESTER RHODES

AT GLOUCESTER BAY
Sonnet without Rhyme

Sea-shells, indigo, inlaid with pearl,
a royal china set so blithely scattered
here among the rooted rocks that view
this fragile elegance with unconcern,
the tossed-out treasure of a spuming sea.
The undulating flight of gulls above
white-crested waves; the wayward winds distending
womb-like sails; and on the crowning hills
twin towers of the proud ancestral church
whose glowing Virgin beacons fishermen
to haven on the sea-shell studded sands.
What sunlit dreams lie shining in these pearl-
encrusted plaques of indigo, bright hopes
and visions shattered by the seething sea!

FATALITÉ

"Elle leur avait donné l'espérance."
Anatole France

Better were those sodden days of dull
Tranquillity, of half-hued melody,
The quasi-orchestrations of my life.
Chiaroscuroed dimness touched with somber,
Sober brush the canvas ambience
Where melancholy habitude depicted
Steady time, for there, there was no hope,
O raging demon, who by brandishing
Ecstatic visions elevates hypnotic
Castles founded on the sliding sand!

I miss that hazy, mournful room, complacent
Satisfaction of my unfelt tears,
That unlit room which had not opened yet
To joy, or fear, or flaring, flaming dreams,
To beauty, fatal, like a falling star!

170

FRANK R. RICHTERS, JR.

CAVALRY REVISITED

Black Orpheus pulled up his stockings
        while the
Veiled Madonna let down her hair
        amidst the turbulence
of a moving train
        bound for
        Mourning Town,

Chaste virgins surrounded
        the coffin
While the Green Berets
        blew taps
to the many multitudes
        gathered upon the
        hill of Death,

The deed was over
    the Man was laid
        in Heaven for all
           eternity to see and
             speculate

The last train left from Mourning Town
        carrying
An ungartered Orpheus
        who met
An unveiled Madonna
    and together
        they went South
           where all was quiet
           and very
             peaceful.

ARTHUR RIMBAUD

Translated by Enid Hester Rhodes,
from the ILLUMINATIONS.

TO A REASON

One tap of your finger on the drum
discharges all sounds and begins
the new harmony.

One step of your foot,
and new men arise
and march on.

You turn your head: the new love!
You turn back — the new love!

"Change our lots,
destroy the plagues,
beginning with time,"
these children chant to you.
"Raise up, it matters not where,
the substance of our fortunes
and of our desires,"
they beg of you.

Arriving from eternity,
you will depart
everywhere.

METROPOLITAN

Along the indigo strait to the seas of Ossian
on the rose and orange sands
tinged by a peach-wine sky,
crystal boulevards rise and cross,
suddenly occupied by young, poor families
whose food comes from the greengrocers' shops.
Nothing affluent — the city!

Along the asphalt desert
helmets flee in headlong rout to the sky:
helmets, wheels, ships, rumps;
armies in flight under sheets of smoke
echeloned in eerie bands.
The sky, befouled by the grieving Sea's
most deadly night-tainted fumes,
swirls round, recoils and sinks.
— War!

Look up:
this arched bridge of wood;
the last vegetable gardens of Samaria;
these masqueraders illuminated
by the lantern lashed at by the frigid night;
a foolish water sprite in the river's bed,
                        her noisy robe;
phosphorescent skulls amid the seedling peas —
and other phantasmagoria —
the countryside.

Roads bordered by trellises and walls
scarcely restraining their woodland groves;
and the fearful flowers you'd call hearts and sisters;

Damask damning by length —
possessions of story-book aristocracies
from beyond the Rhine, Japanese, Guarani,
still suited to receive ancestral melodies —
and there are certain inns
that never open anymore and never will —
there are princesses,
and if you are not too overwhelmed,
the study of the stars — the heavens.

The morning when, with Her,
you struggled in the sparkling snow,
green lips, bright ice, black flags and azure rays,
and the purple perfumes from the Polar sun —
the source of all your strength.

DAWN

I embraced
the summer dawn.

Nothing was stirring
before the palace walls.
The waters lay lifeless;
encamped shadows clustered
on the woodland road.
I stepped forth, rousing currents of air,
alive and warm;
and precious gems marked me well
and wings rose up
without a sound.

My first encounter in the path,
already glittering with cool, pale glints,
was a flower
that told me her name.

I laughed at the flaxen-haired waterfall,
dishevelled across the pines:
on the silvery summit
I espied the goddess.

One by one, I lifted the veils:
in the garden lane waving my arms;
across the plain, where I warned the cook
of her coming.
In the sprawling city
she darted through steeples and domes;
and running beggar-like
across the marble quays,
I gave her chase.

173

At the crest of the road,
near a laurel grove,
I overtook her with her voluminous veils
and sensed somewhat
the vastness of her body.
Dawn and the child plunged
to the bottom of the wood.

Awakening,
I saw it was noon.

ALEX ROBINSON

Sometimes when a singular passage of great poetry,
music or sculpture speaks, with that unique force of love, to me
across centuries, through a strange language or a block of stone,
resurrecting mysteries of beauty from lifeless hieroglyphs,
I seem to hear that artist's plucked soul (hung
briefly in the universe between birth and death)
vibrating in the innermost regions of my mind, unbelievably
intimate. For a long, long moment I sit
absolutely still, listening;
every nerve registers its harmonic to this symphony silent as a sunset,
and I am quite
unable
to move.

BEYOND LONG

It is true I've long been in a strange country,
far away where we are broken-tongued foreigners;
I listened, listened, listened
to life not mine;

it is true I have lived too long alone
like a child's top standing passionately on end,
gyrating, spinning, twisting, swaying
about itself;

it is true that I long for your supple body,
transfixed by those curves of your breasts and hips
swirling in concentric circles
around center;

but it's a shaft of blue from your eyes, meeting mine
momentarily (ringed by a red smile and dark hair),
that touches something in me
beyond long.

174

ALPHONSE ROMAINE

TO PATRICIA

The night, my love, with unrelenting speed,
    is closing in on me.
Am I to be denied the warmth of your smile
    in the twilight of my life?
Am I never to delight in the warmth of your
    kisses, my naughty coquette?
Am I never to delight in your all consuming
    love?
Oh my love, why do you torment me so, for
    you are the sweetness of my youth.
Come to me and tarry for a moment, before
    the wings of Persephone carry me
        off into the night.

J. DAVID ROSS

TRUTH

A man in white
Perched upon a
Marble pedestal
Looked down at the
Humble masses
Seated on the ground
Around him.

"Now is the time,"
He said
"To forget
What plagues us."

"But we can't."
Cried the masses on the ground.

"Try", he said
Giving them the sweet
Absinthe,
And they drank and
They forgot
And were joyous once again

And he murmured
From the marble pedestal
"Fools, who grovel in the earth . . ."

175

THE PLAY

A successful one-night stand
Hear the applause!
They wept and cried out
During the performance
"Smashing!"

But now it's over.
The players are played out
And the costumes have been discarded.

Backstage
Another scenario unfolds —
A satisfaction at the accomplishment,
The conquest of stage-fright.

Was the stage setting right?
Was the emoting effective?
Did the words sound memorized,
Or were they natural?
Was it really good acting?

Or was it love?

EQUALITY

There was a little girl
Who lived on our street
And her name was Susie Brown,
Appropriately enough,
For she was black.

And we played together —
We played hide-and-seek
And we played house
And we had fun.

But we went our own ways
And grew up
And just the other day
Susie Brown's son was killed
In a tragic accident

And my neighbors
Said, "Who cares, he was just
A nigger."

But I cried
Because I could not forget.

THE AWAKENING

Haunted by popsicle-sunny afternoons
And rainyday solitudes,
I find myself recalling
Endless hours of placid contentment
By a stream, in the autumn-burnt wood
Or spring-drenched marsh.

To live as a youth — to see through youth's eyes.
The world so carefree-big.
Can't imagine the world without me.
Death is absurdity,
Life is a gaming sandlot,
Treeclimbing, whistling
Learning to walk before I can run.

Endless hours but a second to the inquisitive
Imaginative mind, registering all from
Little league mornings to lightning-bug evenings.
I was the center of the universe.

But now as youth passes
And life becomes all too real,
The world, I find, can somehow
Exist without me
The sun will somehow rise.
This reality is a bitterpill,
Just a spoke on a limitless wheel.

The summation of all the beauty and
Ecstasy of man confined to a
Number of drops of a fluid so
Precious, yet so wasted.

RICHARD P. RUBINSTEIN

#177

The blood runs,
Like a madras prophylactic,
The words fly,
Like a feather,
The people run,
Like a child after soap bubbles,
And I stand here,
Crying to no one.

177

#143

Winter walk nite,
The cold bites warmth,
Stars give comfort
To a troubled mind,
Dead leaves insulate
The concrete world,
Man in the distance,
Fleeting reminder,
Of reality.

BARRY S. SANTEE

Nothing was coming
Nothing was going
the river ran between
the banks of rock people
and
the wind blew the dead leaf from life to life
But the metallic melon man
refused to talk
too much has not been seen here for his words

FOUR & SEVEN

The narrow corridors of your mind
disturb
the floating twig on
pools of blood
in dusty plains
While darkness hides itself there
behind locked doors
Persons
find themselves in
tape recorders and purple silos
and
People
hide
in closed manholes
singing
''America''

Visible light of darkness rays
pierces lead-body men
of tabloid heads
Taking away the prism
spectrum of moral concern
that conducts barbaric
war marches
to
sacrifice young gods
of thought

GENEVIEVE SARGENT

THE POWER OF WINTER

I withdrew into the winter of my soul
Brooding
Silent
Alone.

The encompassing walls, of my own design and construction, were
A darkened hut
Neither a refuge
Nor yet a prison,

But the walls shut out the understanding so desperately
Hoped for
Wanted
Needed.

And yet in this time of withdrawn dormancy, there arose
An independence
A strength
A liberation.

ADOBE

How firm you stand
In the hot, hot sun,
Impervious to the Apollo-flame.

Protector of the cool calm shade,
Marred only slightly
By wind-driven sand,

Will you stand eternal as yon stone spires,
Or will you crack, crumble, and fall
With neglect and misuse?

179

REVELATION

The lotus, rooted in mud, passes through water,
and emerges to bloom in sunlight.

From torment and pain, through understanding,
peace and joy are born.

From debasement, through recognition,
one is exalted.

From the mundane, through awareness,
spirit-secrets are revealed.

DO NOT MISINTERPRET

For all you can know of me
Is a fleeting fantasy.
A shadow of the me that was
But is no more.

For I am but a breeze that ripples the stillness of a twilight-
indigo lake,
The last call of a whippoorwill at the fullness of darkness,
The briefly-lingering melody of a guitar,
Or the frailty of a geometric web,
Spider-spun.

Know the smoothness of sanded wood
Caressed by appreciative fingertips.
Tingle in the nostrils at the scent of orange blossoms
Intensified by the moisture of night.
Billow in the sail,
Rounding, in a tangy-salt breeze.

Then can you just begin to know me,
For I am inseparable from the beauty I have known.

EVE SCHEFFENACKER

WE

We would walk in the snow most often,
because there was no protection from a wet neck in the rain
and strolling slowly in the spring sunlight was only for romantics.
So we would walk in the snow,
cushioned against the bite of the cold and wind-driven flakes,
catching flakes to see if they were ripe
and whispering in response
to the hushing of the snow as it filtered through brittle branches.

He never held my hand
except when we waded through the field
where the paths of light from the house windows did not reach
and where hollows, logs and tangled branches
waited silently beneath the snow to catch an unsuspecting foot.

We made snowmen once — a boy and a girl —
but he wouldn't make them holding hands in public.
We built them very close together.

And the nights I had to leave him
I would lie in the snow by the light from the doorway
and make angels to guard him
and he would watch and later thank me for my concern.

We loved the snow together, David and I,
especially when we awoke the next morning
and saw our tracks walk into the field,
very close together.

CYCLE

I

There are those dreams
which come so close to your unspoken fears and hopes
that when you wake
they haunt your thoughts wordlessly
and you find yourself momentarily accepting them as real.
But they remain only dreams,
to be shaken from reality as readily as childhood fancies.
So it was with your going,
I felt it had to be a dream
and would shake my head sharply
to dispel the sense of loneliness it left with me.
But I found instead that there was no dream,
except my hope that there was one.

II

When I knew at last that you were truly gone
I was afraid of the dark.
I had become so used to being accompanied by the thought
that you lived,
that the space beside me would someday be filled at your return,
I cast off any feeling of desolation as temporary.
But suddenly you, and the knowledge of your being
were irreparably destroyed
and my loneliness could no longer be limited by the words,
"Until he comes back,"

and it stretched before me
like a dark, narrow corridor with a locked door at the end.
And so I kept a lamp lit to disperse the darkness
And I could no longer nestle warmly into the darkness of a soft bed,
knowing that you would never be there beside me.

III
Now the darkness does not matter,
nor does the dream that crossed the barrier into reality.
The waiting I knew gave me a purpose
because I knew it would end,
and the things I did to make it pass I did for you,
when you would come back.
But I am no longer trailing toward that unseen objective,
nor am I groping through an endless darkness
toward a door that may conceal a light.
I sit now, in a grey mist,
waiting for no one, longing for nothing,
accepting anything and remembering everything.

SUSAN RUTH SCHIMER

AGE

An old man stood in the dark
Groping for the stairs.
A youth passed and said
"Come, I will show you the way."

Together they toppled
Down the stairway.

ROBERT L. SCHLOSSER

ONE NIGHTMARE

Vague turn of numb vortex,
   telepathic tremor in the ague fox.
      Runners from Coentron bearing
         the dismal banalities of the black street.

   Lanterns of flesh, casting red shadows
         under the tree root.
           Numbered orthodox twinge,
            remorse for Leon.
             Twisting wheel
              a grind so to speak.
              No more room . . .

CATSKILL TRAIL

Pebbles crunching under sodden tread,
rain hanging from dark trees.
Gray grass under ferns,
no delay for dawn.

THREE DAY RAIN

"Like an eye that sees, but cannot see itself."

Crooked wall, fortunes of war in spreading sigh.
Pencil line, boundary of furtive glances out the train.
Laughing laconically, roly poly man in green park.
Tryst of heated over orgasm, red zoo monkey smirk.
Auto parts, none in particular, humming buzz of static.
Walking with Canto, visions of a humid room of ants.
Rye whiskey, prodigy of a spent deer shell by the deer trail.
Big sax, under the dust of attic, a bronze tarnish.
Weeping mist darting from willow to willow, searching.
Documented evidence, olive with an ear.
Observing the cycle of a loan, credit bureau penniless.
Pebbles of frost enveloped in golden sun fuzz morning.
Miner shack, a mountain in the timber ring of hermit day.
Rocket fuel, feed my quest of infinity, thy phantom prevails.
Cobblestone fallout shelters in the urban countryside.
Haunting refrain of derilect begging penny money for wine.
Working the shark tank for laughs at noon relapse.
Circuit of sales rep trom Toledo, motel security.
Kneeling before the pill closet, glass veins razor sharp.
Housing development, lovers waking in cold sweat stillness.
Contemporary peer, sowing his sorry twang of melodic epic.
Postage stamp, air mail coast to coast, clutching bag tricks.
A city bus, speaking fluent french after biting the token.
Construction worker, bruises under the thumbnail.
Linda wants to buy a leper for the raffle prize.
Jagged lines of rust in the grass village.
In the backview is the forboding mother Bomb, ticking.
Three day rain, time to ponder the hunter in dark raiment.

METRO HARBOR

Down below the drawbridge of Eddie's joy,
we three sank into the tired sandhills.
A warped tugboat churned slimy
waters into an oozing froth.
Under the seaweed, diamond castles.

183

JILL SCHULZE

AT DOORS

Goblins bark
  at doors of whores
while out on the road
      two members of human carrion
      sag
            and drink to fill up the
  alltooempty evertoopresent
      void

one belches
  the second yawns
"Wanna go?"
"Yeah, okay."
  and night's dark shack
stomps on their heads
  and they are relieved of their
      consciousness

critics of the yoked-mule
breeders of leaky dusk

they stand, wrinkled
at the door
and lick their gums and beetle nut-stained teeth
    and sink to sleep
  before they enter

THE RISE AND THE FALL

  a glistening tear drops from the
  damp sky's eyes
  clings to a dappled leaf
      momentarily
  then loses grip and falls,
  splinters, shatters
  and is eaten, seduced into the greedy roots
  of the tree it clung to
        and the tree is rotted out
  by the worms of the underground
  whose homes are the burrows

184

dug by the falling rain
    to nourish the leaves
who reach to devour heaven
and end as loam
for seeds to come and
clouds of the future
and dreams of never,
while never is now
and continues forever,
ever as leaves grow,
tears fall, weeping, smiling
        water falls and rises,
           rises and falls

NEVER AMBLED

autumn never ambled in today
    it rushed in a whipping chill
    and kissed with the strength
    of hope and the impact of falling timber,
      no, autumn never ambled,
      autumn bludgeoned in, yet softened

touched me, not the autumn of the
      heart,
        the autumn of the mind, for
it did not resemble death or fatique,
but freshened the yet ripening life
        crayoned bright colored circles
        and spheres in whorling
patterns and nonpatterns

    the sweet scent of dried and snow-distant
      air, heavy
in burnt, dying leaf juice, thick
    in wide-cheeked wind

and it all happened today,
    this autumn that speared me
    and charged into the recesses of
    my dreams and shoved
to make them real
      and pressed to act,
      and held to love,

        no, this autumn never ambled in

DONALD L. SCHURMAN (dls)

ON A NAPKIN

I held a little star
    sparkling, shining, beauty-warm
      In my hand,

And someone said,
    "That little star is needed
    over there
    to guide a lost
    soul home."

So I surrendered the
Star.

I held a tiny raindrop,
    cool, shimmering, lovely
    tear
      In my hand,

And someone said,
    "That raindrop can save
    the life
    of that thirsty soul."

And the raindrop slipped through
My fingers.

I held a small puppy,
    soft, warm, happy life,

And someone said,
    "that puppy is tender,
    you are too rough
    in your love and
    too quick to anger."

So they pried the puppy from
My arms.

All this time —
    (on the left)
I held a bolus,
    hard / soft,
    cold,
    sticky,
      In my hand.

And no one wants it —

    So I guess it's mine.

WHEN?

When the expectant glow
    has died,
And the awaited moment
    has gone
Without the event —

What then?
Is the loss
Worth the cost?

Life is a series of
    unfulfilled expectations.
Wisdom is waiting
    and not tiring;

Love is expecting
    and not caring
    about receiving.

SYLVIA SCUDDER

WIND FIRES

Rearing and thrusting
    Toward a grey cloud frothing, cresting
        running before the wind and
      spilling over the horizon onto the lake
Striking and racing —
    silver mane-strands flicking and stinging,
        cutting the face pressed to the
      throbbing, foaming neck.
Lunging and straining —
    surf lashing, scream of gulls,
        flashing silver legs and a
      savage burst of sunlight
And running, no, flying!
    Roaring darkness, the teeth-clenching joy of
        Movement
    Hooves slashing sand and burning eyes.
Foaming and blowing —
    Swift, pounding trail along a stormy beach
    Tiny silver thread between Heaven and Earth
And deep, warm exhaustion.

A DIFFICULT STAGE

We are the people of
   a - mé - ri - ca.
  United we stand!
       against our president
(with whom, says *Freud*, we identify too closely
    to form a Golly-Gee complex.)
  United! toward a more perfect
     cure for
       athlete's foot.
Look at us, world.
  We're squeaky clean
  Except
  Hey! Don't open that door . . .
  Except:
  Mis-use of public utilities
      (Fire-hoses, recall, repel fires . . .)
  Cruelty to animals
      (Human flesh lacks a certain savor)
  False advertising
      ("Sure, take all you want; just be sure . . . '')
    Shut the door, will ya?!
We are the people of a - mé - ri - ca —
    What would They think?

 About divorce rates?
     Hospital ships.
 About water pollution?
     Plows that *CARE*.
 Foreign intervention?
     Student exchange.
   The American Woman — *JA!*
    Who has mastered the art of crying with
      uptilted chin
    (so as not to smear the mascara, dear)
a - mé - ri - ca.
  Who will polish the mirror of your
    smoggy skies
  and make you *see* again?

We, the
  — *You* —
   People
    — *And I* —
  of A - mé - ri - ca.

OF BLACK AND WHITE

Darkness
    A flame is glowing — Speak softly, Satan!
Steel on steel — a chain of hate and
        Dogs.

Black rabbit, white rabbit
    Hush baby, Ma cain't say that.

So we shout
    And they sing
And we kill — oh, God! their children.

Satan is laughing — white rabbit, black
As our souls become dark.

Black rabbit, white rabbit
    Hush baby, Ma don't know either.

FIRE AND ICE

Like an ice-candle I hold you in my body;
    The truth of your words and the beauty of their
        Simplicity
Sears the flesh from my body and the
    veil of my soul curls back like
        Charred paper.

Like melted candle wax your life slips from mine
    and freezes into
      Twisted
        Spirals of
          Memory
    in the infinite Agony of Time
            without.
You will take your brief light from the eyes of my Soul and I,
    the Fool,
    shall stumble for a moment in the shadows of my
        Pain.
Yet that pain, leaving me incomplete, has burned my spirit.
And that spirit, having healed will perhaps,
    someday
Hold a deeper joy for a brighter candle.

189

RICHARD SEBESTA

A DAY AT THE CLUB

Golfers are catholic;
Mass daily twelve till three;
Pin-holding caddies count strokes
as Gethsemane monks rehearse
our Calvary:
"Eli, Eli, lema sabachthani?"

Mulligan . . . God,
ecce homo;
". . . lead us not into sand traps,
but . . ." allow us our trespasses:
Your thirst craves vinegar;
Ours — a dry martini;
Gloria in Escelsis

For the fine round:
we drive while You hang,
pausing at the ninth hour
to replay our bogeys
Dei gratia.

ALAN SHAMOON

. . . AND THE HOUSES OF IVORY SHALL PERISH

From atop your white-capped mountain home I fell
To the earth below, where you are not known to men
And suffered not from the fall, but from the push to Hell
And having to live, once more, with only men.
But I have tasted something much too rare
To eat once more of that on which men are fed;
For so long as I have flown in that air
The red pomegranate would I prefer to bread.
But, alas, no longer do I know if what
I eat is pomegranate or bread or nectar,
Nor do I know if I fell, or if I was
Pushed by you, or if I was ever there.
     I look at the mountain's top and see only
the Heavens above, the Earth below, but, not me.

THE MESSIAH

Yesterday the Friend told me of it lying dead
on the beaches' white sands, beneath the ripe green
bulrushes, a prophet born to death, said
he, mortal in his thoughts, unclean
as sand, who desired to see from behind
his Godlike clouds, God, face-to-face with him.
I went down to the beach where lay kind
saviour, his wings pinned back, and clean
upon his decayed head a jagged piece of thorn entwin'd
in the down, washed up by the salty tide —
Man's wrath crowning Man's god.

The sky, like the water, was blue: It was pure,
and beneath it a flame, angry and small, reaching
with its hot sweating arms into the azure
infinity above, flying into the cold singing
of red water and Ahib blood and death and life
and remembering an earlier encounter with satan's daughter.
He also remembered the falling brackish water canonize
him, wash into his sins, into the wood, into which
he was held by a piece of metal bond from earth.

A swift leap into the sky, a breath of silvery air
stinging in his foaming lungs; and up there,
stunning him as he soared, the ball-of-flame
danced red before his eyes while the coolness of the blue
claimed his soul; and here at last he touched God
and could see him face-to-face.
Now, having felt God, he, thus suspended in space,
was dragged to the coldness of his nest in the sand
to suffer a damp death.

YUDDHA

I sleep, I wake: Which is which — I don't know.
The sky is always poised close to earth — in
Me they touch: the sky far away and low
Dips between a quilt of craggy crops, almost akin.
That is what makes black, God told me,
And whatever else makes not black, makes white.
But now when he shows me his work I see
That black is the day and white is the night.
Strange that I should be troubled with what shouldn't trouble me
(a gadfly in me, stinging, hurting, where it should not be)
All alone neither the strength nor will have I
To mend the wings of a bird that'll kill and still never fly.
    A falcon's shriek and death's seal upon the sky,
With these things I know I will be made to die.

191

JEANNE SHANNON

JOURNEY THROUGH VIRGINIA

Spring
Under the wild plum trees in the windy spring
Smoke from the wash-fires,
Zinc tubs from Wheeling Steel.

Summer
Plum-tree
Peach-tree
Gold of the honey-bee;

Fire-fly
Dragon-fly;

Dusk . . . dusk . . . dusk . . .

Autumn
In the bell-deep dark,
In the dream-
    swollen afternoon

Time passes
Soft as a cat and
    more
        quiet.

SUSAN SHEPARD

sunlight shuffled off
leaving a stark raving nakedness
        (in the glass rain
        splintering through a
        shattered window)
laughing seeing
paper flowering faking
        (withering and crumbling
        in a pile of past
        reeking subjectively dead)
and now that
raving laughing naked stark
        suicides to protest
        mass murder in the
        cultured cremation of essence

192

JACK SMITH

Here is the god of wind and thunder
Poised above the mountain peaks
   Flowing robe
Dances above the tearing winds
The screaming birds
Shooting through the void
   Sword of Sadamune
Slashing through the world
   Lightning and wind
Laughing above the cloud peaks
   Crystal World
Lies all shattered
Black blood flowing from rent mountains
And mind too
   Falls severed
Rolling, Rolling

WINTER LANDSCAPE

Chora walks alone in the winter landscape
Silver drops
Suspended from his nose
  Chora walks,
Swinging a bent stick
At the crescent moon
Icicle like, banging in the sky
  He laughs,
Its image shattered
In the flowing stream
Its crazed surface
A jagged piece of ice . . .
  Chora walks on:
      Into a still pervading expanse
      Of fallen snow
      And each print of his foot
      Can be traced
      Leading into the void —

                                  Out of the picture

PASSING OF THE TAIRA

The seasons melted upon each other
In tonal progression
Under summer hillsides
They passed in quiet meditation
Waiting for the tolling of the temple bell
At evening

MARK I. SMITH

SONNET II

You've known this man in laughter agonize
How dark the dawn, how still the darkness lies.
You know the bitterness his eyes conceal,
The tenderness no sigh nor smiles reveal
Though his soul tear in silence to remain,
Though his heart rage in mute despair insane.
All this you know, all this, and yet your smile
In coldness mocking never ceases, while
Disconsolate his soul uncaring grows
And now no longer love nor pity knows
Or cares to know. Even the soothing pain
Of solitude, once scorned, now's sought in vain.
You have denied him summer warmth and breath
Of spring, and now will you deny him death?

DOES ONE, DARE ONE . . . ?

Does one, dare one, when the slanted light reveals
and thoughts run rampant through your brain of what must be,
when heavy-handed silent darkness steals
the streaming light so you no longer see
the anger and the grief that my heart feels
to see our life turn brown in memory;
when whiteness cools your forehead and you sigh
softly sinking in your blackened sleep,
though holding fast to me as if also I
could fight the ash and gloom to keep
you clean; when incense and black lace defy
what's left of light — does one, dare one weep?

194

JOEL E. SOLKOFF

A WOMAN IS A WOMAN,
BUT A CIGAR IS A GOOD SMOKE

The light glares;
and somehow it's a reminder
of the thought that's bound
there
on top of the shabby wooden bookcase
that says
tomorrow is always better than today —
heaven is just around the corner
under the next hill.

But with you,
I've found today
the death
of that glorious pursuit
penned somewhere in the volume
by a Jefferson
who's never met you.

He seems to say:
my pipe never smokes so well
as the next puff should

would I have cleaned it more
or reamed the bowl better,
had fresher tobacco
or perhaps a better mixture,
had I bothered to fix the bit
or to puff the briar
more slowly
and with more deliberation.

But with you,
because I care,
I do not worry;
I always get
a sweet smoke.

L. DAVID SPARENBERG

IN BETWEEN
(to the people of israel)

a muse in the fields
hidden by the wheat
dodging behind trees — snickering
in the east
the trumpeter plays slow sad music
in between
asphyxiation and revival
sound of a fly buzzing
wings rotating
against the air
he darts
through broken structures
the nicks in village walls
the women work faster
gathering the harvest
the masons — the carpenters
have returned
they build
but do not believe it
"where is my husband
my jonah"
a young bride says
the hammers swing
the saws bear down
now and again
a head jerks up
a fist clenches the air
there is no one
a flock of birds
startled into flight
by a homebound mouse
the faun skips over
rough lip-hair tracks
leading out to the bay area
he laughs softly now
along the new front
the fly imitates
a persistent vulture
circling the desert sun
. . . peace . . .

HAUNTING

my eyes
      would not break
if dropped
      they are steel
i come home
      finding them there
on the kitchen table
      as they were left
they have fought out the day
      breathing alone
with the clock tick
      of every second
pointing toward the door
      watching for your return
i would go over
      pick them up
and place them
      back on the shelf
let the dust gather
      everything else about me
screams
      — no more —
— it is over —
      but my eyes
tense and hard — wait
      grabbing the open strands
of love
      spilling out boulders
two by two
      on the broken floor
soon i will be piled in
      buried
under a mountain
      of hot pear-stones
i tell them
      with wet anxious hands
— come away now —
      — the vigil is over —
— we must avoid the past —
      — in a winter of sleep —
but they won't budge
      the brave solitary eyes
still alive with a dream

of your lips speaking
—hello darling—
　　　　—i've come home again—
they just hang up
　　　like proud nations
snarling at the weakness
　　　of my defeated heart

TO J. S.— IN MORNING TEARS

straining through the window-bars
braces between the squares of glass
criss-crossed patterns retaining me
sectioning my haggard features
i feel the dark lines press against me
my eyes break out
and scamper across the gray yard
in the raining morning air
i see you standing below me
under the crumbling tower
head tilted up—waving smiling . . . hello
the imported sunlight
cascades you—fiery madonna
the wind-horse flies you up to me
we touch in the middle of low clouds
in my foggy mind
my hands recoil and attack me
bleeding at the ends—violent
tiny sore mouths of your name
i realize my face is wet and broken
weeds nesting pale lips
explode on my jungle-cheeks
something alive kicks in my head
near the top—to escape
i stumble back dizzy and awkward
repulsed from the standing bars
strike a broad edge and slide down
my prison holds me with brutal arms
the walls delighted with their power
the ceiling stomps on me
quickly passing the bed i grab a pillow
drag it with me to the floor
i lay there sprawled over myself
knotting and chewing the case
trying to sleep without you
captured in a hideous dream

FIRE

the face of the earth
cries up to me
i am rich with pines
i've shaved from her head
the hair endings hinge before me
separate and bleeding
in a moment
i've cut across her heart
and left deep scars
turned her old over night
for years she will go about
digging living bodies
from the charred ruins
leaves come after me
scraps of blazing flesh
my name is on her
my fortune in precise numbers
plowed into her forehead
the face of the earth
cries up to me
and i tramp over her dispassionately
one foot tearing the mouth
the other gouging in her eyes

CONTEMPORARY POEM

in the cold perfume of your eyes
i see the moss-covered nation
green guardsmen — washing to me
angry and gritting their teeth
the winestained grass parts
the forest sleeps like a battlefield
of ash-pit pines and trash can maples
the sandy beach is invading
tight against my pacifist cheeks
there in a thousand miniature impressions
are the cities of jesus and buddha
ashes set on fire again
suffering the torments of another persecution
you are killing the people of love
in the handsome streets of new eden
where i first met you — a prophetic caesar
where you ordered me in
so your bullskin lashes could beat me

199

and the curling needles of your head
could molest my convictions
as i come back from the sea of injustice
ashamed of what you are doing
the fragrance of your right-eyed gaze
comes back — patroling the groaning shore
the patriotic muse of war
ready to break out swinging his fist
against the breast of children

FRANCIS C. SPATARO

KARMIC LOVE

I know not the color of your hair,
    Nor of your eyes
Or your gait, or the physical form
    Of your recurring soul
Which I know well since we were
    Lovers long ago
Over-There and Here when we recurred.

It's just your body I don't know
    Your face, your voice, what clothes
      To expect,
What costume your angelic whim will pick;
Yet we shall meet . . .
    We must Over-There and Here
      For we are one
    In Karmic Love.

SALVATORE FRANK SPIEZA

PASSING THOUGHT

Life is a Merry-go-round, with love as its motor.
The past is dead, the future unimaginable, with no
escape.
Nothing your own, except a few cubic inches inside
your skull.
You're in love, but it's only a passing thought.
To be exceeded by something more beautiful, and
glorious.
Only to be torn down by reality, after the thought
leaves your disabled mind.

A single human creature is nothing without love;
to live in solitude is cruel, to love is worse.

Because to be annihilated by something you love is
worse then death by solitude.

Even as you try to nourish the thought from its
death, you alibi her evils and selfishness.

You recall the past, and get flash backs of joyful
visions.

If only you can recall the pain and hurt as vividly
as you felt it.

You would let each passing thought be a lesson
rather than a wanting memory of something that can only
exist in your interthoughts.

WILLIAM STABOSZ

FIVE POEMS

An enthused sincere man
Did his unofficial job
Too well
So the authorities
Having no jurisdiction over
This unofficial office
Took some sticks
A match
And one enthused sincere man . . .
And they fired him

Softly
feet whispering to the pavement
Turbulent winds
whistling through my nostrils
while my heart pumps enough
to keep six men alive
I'm searching
For what the ages have lost
and I've never found whole
or sensed too much
Although I don't know it now
I will when I find it.
When I find it.
What?

Listen!
Softly from the pulpit,
"Blessed are the peacemakers."
With conviction from the politician,
"Peace! Peace is what we want."
The citizens, students —
    the massive voice,
"Stop the war."

(sometimes we mean what we say)

The self evident message
Echoes down the bleak pit
Called history
    and fades . . .

Too soon the ignorant silence
Is filled anew by the clamor
Of the living ignorance
That fearsome monster
The war
The living death
(Resurrected)

Man came from the animal
Approaching greater life
(so he claims)

Yet even to this day
Our actions scream the truth
Of the wretched belief
Which shame won't let us voice
(shame, ignorance, and willful hypocracy)
"The right to life belongs to
Him who has the strength to
Seize it."

The lesson of love's
a hard one to grasp.
To even the most diligent students
a stern subject.

Only by straining
closing an eye to scattered facts
do we find hope
for this race of schoolboys
So pitifully, thoroughly distracted.

Between my tears comes the oppressing question
Will we ever learn?

202

Comfort of the womb
While the world
Weapons in one hand
Bandages in the other
Invites me to a sore happiness.
Calling out,
"I dare you to face me,
to try and love me.
I dare you to be born."

Nobody, not even herself,
Except for everybody,
Made the strumpet.
Somehow (it happened
mysteriously, like everything else)
and unfortunately
A human being
A real woman
Became undone and died.
Nobody important ever said,
"Love thy hooker as thyself."
Nonetheless I believe it.

D. STACY

THE CIGARETTE

A huge hand lifts it from the pack
Round and slender by machine's miracle
To his lips it goes and awaits death
Zip! the flame approaches, ah, birth

The first drag is always the best
Smoke swirls about aimlessly
Rising high into the air to nonexistence
Tobacco bits are spit out on the floor

A moment to savor the fine taste
And then into the ashtray
Where it will await another puff
But the huge hand and welcome lips depart

Slowly it burns down
Once four, now only two
The stream of smoke never breaks
Ceremoniously the ash lengthens

Soon it is all ash
And then the stream breaks
Death has come, inevitable as it was
And there is nothing as the ash is blown away

JEFF STEARNS

she flew
    from the corner
    her hair
wet and stringy,
        running
        penetrating the
                    rain
                    pour
            to miss
    the puddle
            or the
                        soggy garbage
            on the
            brick street
            makes
    her coat
            swing
                        to show
            her
    s
        undress
            which was so
                        inappropriate
        for
        today

R. WAYNE STEDINGH

THE SWANS OF LAKE NEUCHATEL

A streamlined wisp of purity,
The ethereal spirit of air;
A flash of ruddy in the nose,
A rapid bending of wings paired;
A hissed ker-plunk, a folding sigh of down:
The swan perplexed is calmer now
Though the heart beats quick as the storm
Still rages on the lake.
A society, now, of heart beats beats
In time to rising swells.

And a society away upon the rocks,
a less fortunate companion.
Where rocks grow sharp, where waves spit foam
And the wind hurries,
Lies a fractured beak and a bloody eye
On a field of crumpled white.

TO MAKE A GENIUS

To make a genius takes much mystery,
Two hundred pounds of mist,
A lot of envy,
And a psychiatrist.

I'LL TELL YOU HOW THE POWDER PUFFED

I'll tell you how the powder puffed
Upon a wrinkled face:
A peep of phosphorescence, a fit of orange ire;
A peeling tangerine that shot
Its nectar in the eye.
It was a gold complexioned monogram
For all the race to wear.

A particled profusion poised
Above mascara'd grace,
A cloud of castigation formed
And multiplied the air;
The bomb of powdered elegance
Had slapped upon the brow.

A voice cried out unrecognized
Brought sneezes from the crowd.

THE CITY

The old man cried to the city:

    we are not Gods
    nor statues of men
        but passion flowers
        waiting to be stabbed
                and kissed

and the city said:

    on your knees
    and I will stab . . .

EUROPA AND I

Europa and i
    are waiting for the Iceman to come
    we are awaiting the Second Coming
and we are waiting for the yellow Phoenix to really burn
so the Sphinx-faced
    lion of tomorrow can come roaring in
    on the ticker-tapes
    and bite the heads off johnny doe.

But there's a bunch of push-button babies
that must a' been popsicle kids
        one time
who are trampling out the cool grape vintage
    of their dads
    who denied them then
    who are the yellow cats today
    takin' it easy
    they say
    with their mechanical boom-booms and tom-toms.

And i lean over to Europa
an' ask 'er if that's the beauty of the lilies
    and she is silent
and all i can hear is the snare drummers raping
    the animal skin
and mine eyes can see the glory comin'
    wearin' a DARn Good Citizenship Medal
over his heart.

LE PRINTEMPS DES JURAS

The lilacs now are blooming on the way
To school, and every day I pass I look
Envying the red faced man who owns them,
Fathered and mothered them with his green thumb.

All autumn I watched the owner prune and wrap
Their supple sides in cages of burlap,
— Probably thinking: It will keep them warm.
But are Nature's children weak and sickly?

All winter they were so encased and filled
With snow. And then in March the foen came
And ripped the brown bags off their trembling pegs,
Bent the slender twigs, and loosed their prisoned heads . . .

Or nearly so. Now the air intoxicate
With purple breath brings my face to purple hue
As lumbrous Alpine walls constrain their spread,
Gulp the fragrant beauty that would louder speak,

And dimly stare, challenge with Alpine dare,
Desire to grasp the bough's sweet-scarlet mistress,
To breathe that breath that breathes. My hand leaps up.
A screendoor bangs. And I am caught red handed.

THE CONTENTED DOMESTIC.SIGH

I am delighted
    drinking orange juice for breakfast
    and fumbling with milk cartons
    under blood-shot eyes in the morning.

I should be satisfied
    pulling weeds every year from the lawn
    just so I could plant tulips once in a while
    and watch the rainbowed lawn sprinkler
    dazzle green grass growing / and spudder gravel patches / spudder.

I am fulfilled
    filling the plastic bucket with hose water
    washing the car on Sunday afternoons.

I am so pleased
    with wifey and my family / so
    all we need is an atomic bomb in the back yard.

207

JOHNNY SARTUS

Johnny Sartus, I hate you
jammed down people's throats
like pablum or dogfood.
Your brand of victuals is too damned
rich for our digestive tracts
. . . even for the hardy Swedes.

A new Palace of Just playgrounds?
Just playin' around again
the idea of truth and justice
where beaten flesh napalm blessed
makes the eye naked for all to see
it is in ourselves, not in our stars,
that wear under things
greater than our stars
following the Judas goat,
leading ourselves democratically to the Cross.

A. BROOKE STEPHENS

PHOENIX

nothing so many times
I have found at night's end
driven by memory's backward crawl
spun about by dross-ends
meandering half-thoughts of youth's confusion
the butt-ends of abstraction's delusion

loneliness too many times
I have found in faded rooms
where light bulbs stare back
and mirrors do not retract
as eyes meet eyes in stranger's parting
and the pounding of a heart
marks the illusive thread of time

comes the dawn as the roach flees
startled from fitful dreams and
morning on its back, belly up, greets me
beckoning like a warm night's whore
to sweat stained sheets whispering
harm and weeping last night's anguish
or muttering the lost words of old men

208

that absently grip withered lives
bewildered by the cold silent steel
that we have become

but morning will yet be mine
and night shall bruise and pucker my lips
no more with false promise
buried deep within me
is a furious and insistent throb
the hiss and flow of my sweet red life
across dark plains I am a hungry wind
with fiery hands I grope and
burn to savage rhythms

STUART STEWART

THE MAN

His youth, he claimed, had left him in an age
Of unforgotten, too forgotten dreams.
Of time too swift that passed him as he strayed
Into a thousand paths of flowered streams.

Into a life amidst a world he shunned
Had dropped his birth unwanted from the sky;
Had sensed the senseless being he'd become,
And driven youth to age from youth's reply.

Had sought in vain the sun who's rays repelled,
From distant and unmeasurable heights,
The promise he'd believed that life had held:
Of flower's bloom in artificial lights.

In solitude on sand with dampened grains
From rain which dropped from clouds that hid the sun,
Into a world of populated strains
Had left behind a song to be unsung.

The Man sang
In a tuneless world.
He walked where steps were useless,
And his feet betrayed
The purpose of his life.
The Man lived with every man and woman.
The Man died
Alone.

PATRICIA STOLFA

HOMING

We have been in this place before.
But it was still more before
When eyes were kitten-closed.
We knew the rocks, the gulches here before
By wandering, rushing, stumbling
To muddle slowly, hurtly back.
Yet that was more before.
With our separately paired eyes still sealed,
And only
The sometimes warm, mostly clutching hands,
We separate twinly took,
There was reason then to the bleed.
It hurt in that before, but after
Tore honeyed separately paired lids
Apart.

We saw each other, wanly smiled each other tears.
Slowly, weakly, but one quartet of separately paired eyes,
We turned: the vista acknowledged our steady, four-eyed gaze.

The first before expired then,
Defining in its death
A thousand and one of its brothers,
A thousand afters,
Plus an eternal now.

Why have we come to this place again,
Wandering, rushing, stumbling its gulches, rocks,
Here after before?
Gasping now, winded,
After before,
Choking on sand-stung desiccated air
That sucks from us more life-strength
Than we from it life-element.

Four steady open eyes are not enough.
Unlovely Love, we slough again the wasting sand
To sear ourself another after.

We will come to this place again,
After this burning after.

210

ALAN F. STONEBRAKER

CONFLICT OVER LOBSTER

"The trouble with our society"
she said,
cracking a claw
"is that not enough people
want to do noble things."

"The trouble with our society"
he said,
eliminating the last
of his vodka
"is that too many people
want to do noble things
rather than do things nobly."

LINDA

She cried
   silently
  softly

as she told him
   i love you

and he made an attempt
   firmly

allrightthen
   whileiamgone
   getoffcontraceptives
   anddonotgotobed
   withanyonebuteddie

She cried
   silently
  softly

and refused.

211

ODE: THE AMERICAN DREAM

to not e.p. but t.s.e.
truly il miglier fabbro

Lodge member;
have a bazaar
covered dish supper
Donate
cast off dresses for old ladies
old dresses for cast off ladies.

A standing ovation
kiss an ass
slap a back or two
"Have a cigar"
   or a drink
     or
       something

"We don't go for that stuff"
   of course we don't

"Yessir, a fine young ballplayer"
will surely make it
will probably make her
might make them all

A world of keys
   house key
   club key
   go to Wa-ki-key
   Phi Beta Kappa key
key
     to the city

key to success

SUCCESS

SSECCUS

S*S*S*C*C*E*U*

Go to college
"sure thing"

212

Grow mature
        of course
. . . but . . . in an incubator
slightly sterile.

Fornicate
        of course
at least 95% we are told
(but that's in nice schools)

Figures slightly higher in the East.

Daily prostitution
    of self ?
    of ideas
        and
            ideals

Hourly dissection;
turned inside out
cleansed
lavaged
    flushed

    Then
refilled
filled up
sown up.

Make The Adjustment

too bad you couldn't

Classified
he said "pinned and wriggling to the wall"
"would you rather be a garbageman or . . .
    but wait
        if you lust after your mother go to question #13"

They said "God is dead"
HA,HA,HA,Ha,Ha,ha,h. . . . sorry
yes, yes, that's true   (last tuesday it was)
certainly is true   (knew his father)
too bad (nice boy)

You said "I'd rather be a legend"
        can't make the grade, eh?

Pillar of the community
    love thy neighbor as thyself

. . . but . . . don't bend over neighbor.

213

D. G. STUBBS

SORRY 'BOUT THAT, GOD
Three Poems

The Master showed me how
    it worked
Until I tried —
      things burst
      rain fell
      waves crashed
All shattered in a shower . . .
      He did not come again.

I laid a stone upon my head
      and called myself a Christian
All knelt to grab their stones
      and all rushed to join me
Too soon there were too many
      and arguments ensued
In disgust some threw their stones
      and struck the others down
It turned into a crusade
      and later none knew why
The meaning was forgotten
      and the stone became a stone.

God is there
      we've listened to
          rain — thunder — wind
      we've done for
          good — sacrifice — salvation
          but
Our prophets erred
      crusades failed
          temples crumbled
Today we bury God . . .

214

ARTHUR S. TAMKIN

THOUGHTS OF HOME

It was too late to hear the rustling of maples
Through the parlor windows, yet I knew
The leaves were blowing, for empty rooms told me so.
The echo of my whisper nearly reverberated
into a rising crescendo, as other voices,
long forgotten, renewed an ancient tete-a-tete.
Improvising upon hauntingly familiar themes,
They played a glisando with an unhurried ease,
And reminded me that this was home.

Father tried to fix the window sash, but soon
He retired to that slower, inner peace
Purchased with cigar smoke and aperitifs,
While, dying a little deeper, he dreamt of
Yesterday.
Mother remained cheerful as termites
Bored into the beam, undermining the foundation.
And, sister weeping, I marched off to war.

The moon set out its golden lantern, bathing
The sideboards in a pale hue, and catching
My shadow transfixed upon the parlor wall.
Schooled in dying, I strained to catch
The echoes of the voices, voices sighing,
Sister weeping, and the deft variations
on a moonlit theme.

MYRON TAYLOR

SEA GLASS

The Funeral
    Crystalline
       revolt against man
silent laughter
      made to be broken
    tossed on some rocky shore
  pseudo-world
      fingers brush blood
pale
     figures dimly seen
   sad song of flute

Ice
    sterile
        weeping not heard
Silent bird feathers
        rustling
            silence

The Death
    Stone
        stick
water
    water
        stone
            stick
water
    water
        silent birds flapping
above
        below
    Black rocks
    tap . . . tap . . . tap
golden fishes
        frozen
    sea birds walking
crash
    purple
        thundering abyss
little black boxes
    shut

The Birth
    Wanderers, Wanderers
salt eaten into
    not smooth
        an infinite
Black rocks
            labyrinth
    not clear
Silent birds stalking
    tick . . . tock . . . tick . . . tock
        frosted patina
seablown
    still
        night
pseudo-world
        fingertips grip sand
    warm

```
                        sea change
            motionless
                  wild
                      free —
                          false
```

B. S. THOMPSON

OGUNQUIT

O winters dim-med moon, slushed in clouds —
            hollow-eye, circled infinity
holy halloween; under homosexual's walk,
                              wolf croons —
O summer fullness, in you do shine —
            so narrow is the intimate romantic mind,
listen to winter's wolf cry;
            cast the shadow of the walking homosexuals —

O winter's summer moon, intimate is infinite . . .

THE BEAT

The City — streets wet from rain;
                  a gay pattern is formed — cluster of
                  lights reflects in the black base;
my face, somehow consumed in a gayety affair — for a
while my frustration is fascinated —

I feel —

a compelling, a motivation — my desire

that sent me into this rainy street, like a dog in rainy
heat . . .

lonely,

I move the street through; the night with its passion
that felt my stomach out into this rainy night

I know,

the feeling shall die, unsatisfied, and another night
it shall die unsatisfied — unsatisfied and I will die
never satisfied

and the rainy street, such a gayety pattern, that only
reflects the light's peak — I'm consumed unsatisfied . . .

217

THE DIVIDING LINE

Three centuries of row-houses
we walked by across too   acting as lovers seem to others
small smiles   slight head shakes affirming what has been
denied by the world
three centuries of deterioration   standing proof
Who slapped her ass to awaken   I echoed the cry
across state lines I stepped   faces echo echo foot steps
sound All I singled a sound out   from behind centuries I
heard faces that echo like foot steps   we met upon our
eclectic path   sounding out laughter   comes back   from
buildings holding centuries   behind walls   lovers lay gripping across that line that divides the ass   affirming life
feeling flesh succulent sweat   held in their hands
O how I can hear her very words to those she loved in the
past   so well constructed   every brick in place
I cried when the slap felt me alive   born alone gripping to
the dark to the light was known
Tonight I will affirm between the firmament of sight and
sound holding tight upon that line that divides all things
like centuries

SAINTS SPREAD THEIR SILVER NETS

Sonnet No. 2

Yes I, with the wish of a shooting star that came to me
when awakening from my dream; curse their reality — en-
tangled in currents, I the only opponent, a drowning
dream — un-descending in mid-stream; though I must be
careful to evade the awaiting nets, that hide behind weeds.
The sun has been exiled by the darkness, and the fates that
await me are un-seen; all that I fear is here — the moon
brings more dark to the night, calling too the stream to tide
and any hope to escape descends with on-coming un-seen fates
of nature. Now I see saints setting upon their shrines casting silver nets in this child's pond — here no goldfish go;
they hope to catch the corona of that shooting star. Saints
pull in your spread nets; all that sparkles the moon reflects —
go, and sleep upon your dreams let my darkness glow; for in
this pond only ugly swans swim, as all children know.

JOURNEY-MAN

to each his own island and
abandon all hope of rescue —
there is none to come upon
un-firm sand; and I refuse
to put my hand out in dis-
tress . . .

DON TOLL

THE NEW ORDER

In the Forum, perfumed garbage stench
   Gives delicate aroma to gasping marble.
   Metal, slivers of tins oxidized
Besieges fluted columns tinted.

Potato chips, flip-top beer permeated
   Crinkle, wind-whipped and scatter
   Granny Gooselike in marble recesses.

Has Granny Goose been here? Has man?
   In the Land of Sky Blue Waters
   The temples are dying. Pompey was buried.
   Ammo filled the Parthenon. Bomb it.
   Will potato chips feed insectivores?
   Will beerlicks draw roving Gods?

Zeus is dead. Or moribund.
   Or has he become so common?
   Is his beard but a sigh of protest?
   Olympus has been scaled.
   Zeus must rove . . . Granny Gooselike.

OF A CERTAIN SUMMER TIME

She has a love,
   A warm soft love like a summer
   Breath on falling leaves,

And the love falls on me as I lie
   Beneath the wind-blown leaves
   And let them tease my cheek,

And feel the kisses touch against
   My cheek as do the leaves
   And I am happy in the touch.

For it is late summer and the leaves
Are warm and fall in orange
As the sun soothes them,

And I am warm as the kiss caresses me,
Not as a fainting flick of leaf,
But as a soft lingering love.

O, I am bathed in touches of warm-
Hued crispness of falling leaves,
And her love is by my side,

And she is warm and she is soft,
And her love is open to me,
In the soft-breathing summer sun.

PATRICK TOOMAY

SIMPLE I

sometimes, walking alone
in rain
even in the rain
it is cool,   yes
walking alone
it is   just suddenly   now!cold.
oh.
i have no sweater
and no place to go
just walking.

sharp and clear images
are greeted
bright in the gray
backdrop —
dripping leaves   defined
by the dustless air and . . .
walking alone in rain
a lengthy gaze   destructive.

—splashing the evenness   out of the road
ruining new perfection
i watch my face,
shattered with my own feet   and
scattered in a thousand ways
just walking,
emerged in the asphalt's breath
it was once hot.

now it has stopped,
the rain.
the chlorophyll injection
affecting life   takes hold   a
drowsy —dizzy —yellow-jade.
from the shaded mind
an uttered thought:
"my face lies waiting for collection."

MANUEL RIVERA TORRES

PIECES

The bodies fall and
Disintegrate
In insignificant pieces
That break again;
Which break
At their turn,
And those others,
Without any other possibility
Break again,
And those
And the others,
And every piece that remains
Of these filthy bodies
Will continue to break
— Without ever ending —
Because Life,
And bodies,
And people,
Were made to break like that,
Always in pieces,
And pieces,
Until getting lost in the vortex
Of the whole Universe,
That in pieces
— Always breaking —
Integrates and disintegrates
With other pieces,
That also continue to break,
In the irremediable alternative
Of that which —without existing —
In order to appear that it exists,
Has to continue to break
Day after day,
Moment after moment,
Without ever ending . . .

I SAW YOU DEAD

. . . and upon seeing you dead,
So still and
Quiet,
Pale (lying),
Deaf,
Without breath,
I ran as a madman,
I screamed without consolation . . .
And upon getting outside
And looking to the Heavens
I asked in anger
—Almost cursing —
Why did you steal her
God,
Why did you kill her?

I CANNOT OPPOSE IT

I tell myself, in my delirium,
That maybe I am a miracle;
Or perhaps, what was dreamed of
In a Divine Chore.
Maybe I am the Project
That was finally accomplished,
Or, am I perhaps the impossible
Turned into a *being?*
Who knows if I am
That which was never thought of,
That idea claimed by all
Who try
To say that they "already know"
Though truly they have not
Even the limited vision
Of what might be . . .
. . . That is my tragedy:
Feeling that I am *someone*
Knowing that I am living;
Crying because I die,
And however existing;
And though consciously alive
(Or am I perhaps just passing through?)
I resign myself to dying
Since I cannot oppose it . . .

I AM TURNING BLOODLESS

While my heart
Burns
— And becomes ashes —
My delirium goes further,
And the heart beats with strengths
That seem stolen
From *another force*,
That will never be my force,
Because it doesn't fit in me,
Doesn't adjust to my borders.
And that force hurts me,
And I try to pull it out
Because my heart
Has begun to hurt me . . .

My conscience becomes confused.
I fear that it might burst in madness
Because, frightened, I realize
That my hands are becoming
Bloodless;
That my breath is becoming
Bloodless;
That my beat is becoming
Bloodless;
That my delirium is becoming
Bloodless;
That my madness is not madness any more
Because it has no blood . . .
And while my heart
Burns
— And becomes ashes —
I feel burning the Death
That consumes my life;
And my ashes have no blood
Any more either,
And even my blood
Has become bloodless
Finally . . .

GEORGE TRESNAK

MODERN AND ANCIENT LOVE

The torture of eyes that flit
And then dart away
When met
Was less in another day.
Nowadays man must sift
The torment cast his way
To find
The remnant of a ray
Of hope that there is yet
Something he could say
To check
The silent barbs that flay
Through every shrug and shield;
The barbs that never slay
But wound
The feelings that convey,
If told, affection and a claim.
He must plead and pray
That she
Will let the feelings stay.
An ancient on a foreign soil,
Thwarted when he sought to pay
For one
He sought to take away,
Descended on the maiden's town,
Hooves of steed pounding clay,
And swept
Her off amidst arrows' spray.
When in-law band upon his trail
Caused his coat of mail to fray
(With swords,
Consummation to delay)
He held the throng at bay
Though wounded. But comparing his duress
To the other's ,
The ancient suffered less.

DIGNITY

Dignity is not departing from the norm
With adjectives denoting inner storm
When a coin-slotted quarter, dime or nickel
Doesn't produce machine-vent candy, pop or pickle.

Dignity is staying calm and tight-lipped
When you're a nickel, dime or even quarter gypped.
Dignity's resolve to forget the matter pending
Introduction to an inventor of vending.

LOUIS TRIFON

BUS RIDE

Bus ride,
Through the cold and driving rain,
In and out and through my brain,
Drops upon the pane.

Bus ride,
Dark night is all aflame,
Flaming with the gentle name,
Day and night are all the same.

Bus ride,
Lonely streets filled with eyes,
Looking for the dying cries,
Love the life and shun the lies.

Bus ride,
Round in circles in the air,
Back to earth I know not where,
Found is lost and I don't care.

AUDREY VELEBA

THE NUMBER ONE DEGENERATION

Fear is ugly without a face,
Born of ignorance, a disgrace.
He has a grip without a case
And travels at a maddening pace.
Many say he has no place,
But someone always finds him space.
Then he moves in to abase,
The innocent and oppressed minor race.

SPLENDOURA

The midnight Sun is rising beyond the sixty-sixth parallel.
It embraces my awe with inspiring and becomes my magnificent citadel.

A midsummer's phenomenon, the aura of majesty.
My nocturnal never-never land and I its devoted refugee.

ALONENESS

Aloneness is everywhere,

                    v
                a e
riding the w   s of every sea,

Break ing   in clouds of every dawn,

                              t
                    d   p
                    n   e
                    i   w
danglin   on needle tips of w   s   pines,
        g

BeAtInG iN tHe HeArT of someone unloved,

on a w r i t h i n g   face of pain,

after death'   before birth,
                    i
                    n
                    B
                    e
                    t
                    w
                    e
                    e
                    n
          and .

D
  o
    w
        n the beaten path of despair, without difficulty,

                              it is found.

226

TOM WADE

DECADENCE, SI

Up from the gutter walks man-kind with beads with trinkets
with cheap tin rooound its neck with silver bells in pockets
that jiiingle with leather bound feet that underneath the grass
flattens with contempt an obstacle not of the times

Up from the gutter walks man-kind with clothes spuuun from
the land with buttons of pearl with shaades of green jade
with seeds of plenty derived of a past that is now not
of the times

Up from the gutter walks man-kind with socks of yarn with eyyes
bespectacled with forks of sterling silver that carve the
milk-starved-mammal-which-was-once   But
is now of an age that is not of its time

PAUL MALLORY WALKER

VANITY

Squeezing through venetian blinds,
Dust particles play tag, whirl, wind,
Cartwheel on sliced beams of breakfast sunlight.

A cataract of loneliness polarizes
The glow of an April morning.
Time for visiting hours,
A birthday without a card.
I resented the impression game,
But even this was called,
For she was a queen,
Too busy to care
For the little man,
Too young to share
What You have given.

Dewdrops diamond clover,
Catch a jaded ray, rainbow it over
To spring spirits as prism'd beauty.

LABOR DAY — #54

The blink of beams, a screech, then screams,
Phosphorescence, crackling chrome,
Rounds of red on a moaning dome.
Electric winks of *charity* — just dreams,
And Schaeffer scratchings. Statistic fifty-four,
In silent darkness, labors no more.

SANDI WALKER

SEASONS

You know a lot of things that I don't know
but we each feel
the sun
warm on our skin

I'm always lost and looking for my way
sometimes
more intensely than others

I cry and laugh
into the tunnel

the sun looms ahead
I run to it
That is what I have been looking for

I only ask then,
Why do the seasons change?

THOMAS EARL WALRATH

THEIR LIFE

keep walkin down the road,
lookin for your freedom.
you ain't goin to find it,
cause you're the wrong generation.
keep walkin man, keep walkin.
you can laugh at our kind,
but that won't find ya life.
ah, this black world, dark world
will swallow you up,
with no second thought.
let the gray rains

228

fall on your tortured head,
and infiltrate your black thoughts.
god, why do you look for life,
when you ain't even livin?

ELIZABETH S. WALTON

Love is a seven
letter word
with five inflections
and no
meanings
As we stumble
we give
many meanings
many crayons in an empty box.

DEBORAH WEINSTEIN

The whole time I was braiding her hair,
Behind me lurked infinity,
Surrounding my shoulders, playing there.

Ignoring this, and undestroyed,
I braided while I whistled tunes,
Into the greedy, noteless void.

YOUR HANDS

When violets forget they're blue
And memories forget to be remembered;
When the sun dissolves the dew
Before the morn awakes;
And the night forgets how deep
Its blanket is;
When the rivers never seep
Into the patient sea —

Your hands
Will not forget
The where and how
The yes and now
The quick and rain
   Of me.

A CARPETED ABYSS

Tonight I touched my sadness
When I fell into my cave
And found the flame I'd feared
Was just a lamp to light my way.

The demons in my dreams were only
Toys that I had broken long ago,
That lay in disarray among the fog.
(And when I cried, it echoed.)

KATHLEEN WEST

CHERCHANT

The scalpel snowflakes slit the ethered air.
That promiscuous caress
From the hand of loneliness
Sifts numbly on my cheek and hair,
Shroud-silent, fathomless.

Infinitesimal silver-feathered larks
Dart past the candlelight,
Bind the eyes of night,
Strangle the old oak patriarchs
Gently, without a fight.

The near-blind hunter wearily stalks his prey
Above the silent snows,
Tense-listening as he goes
For sounds that presences betray:
Hears silence only. So the darkness grows.

SEAN WILKINSON

MY LOVE COMES IN THE NIGHT AND MOURNING

my love comes in the night and mourning,
weaving darkly past electrocution bed ends,
long hearse fenders brushing close
to arc the blue air.
she is poised to leap behind her,
lay there with her candy smile in the silk
so once and final
in her happy box.

230

CATS' EYES

i am in cats' eyes
and a rain pool
backward;
time and your eye
prismly refract me well
for naming single colors.
see me window imaged,
seen and through,
just lights and shadows,
moving, easing into
fluid wholeness.

DIGRESSION

i might as easily
(easier, much easier)
be dead as here
devirginating
(freud tells us writing,
after all, is the emission
of fluid from a cylindrical
object onto a clean piece of
paper which raises some
interesting questions
about the sexuality
of typing, but anyway)
since i'm not
and since i am
(dead and devirginating
respectively)
i'd like to call
attention *(ATTENTION)* (?)
to a word
(any one, your choice);
pick it up and
throw it down, paint it,
feed it, trim it,
burn it and gold leaf it,
say it again,
in a few minutes
and tomorrow.
isn't it foolish,
the way it sounds
with repetition,
all alone and
helpless.

231

POEM FOR MICHAEL

the coal step sat down
spit ringed,
michael in the t-shirt too
and waited.
city rain in summer doesn't last long.
william's brown dust chest
came gold and amber
chestnut and his wire hair
was hung with mercury as the sun
came past the corner
and the streets steamed.

IS IT A . . .

all of a sudden
(they were sitting
on the ammo boxes)
with hardly a chance
to wave 'hello' or
a flag (walker was
picking his nose)
a big mother bomber
(one of ours, grunt)
gave each one a
napalm enema
(incinerated walker's
nose) but
in the fourth column,
page five, UPI
tells mom (mrs. walker
and the kids as well) ''a
spokesman
said the bombing
mistake
wouldbeinvestigated''

LINDA WILSON

SNOWFALL AND THAW

A sugar bowl upset above our heads,

Heavy, liquid granules parachuting gently down
to crown the peaks and nestle in the valleys
of our oatmeal textured world.

Under the frenzied stirrings of our overboot spoons,
white grains refined to slushy brown sugar lumps.

Impatient Sun, ravenous in the biting cold,
greedily licks up the brown lumps,

Leaving only shady corners with their cowering crumbs
and brown-black molasses coursing through the gutters.

BRUCE WINGO

CAPTAIN

Captain
ruler of the poet's pen
I walked your Camden streets
and saw your dirty Delaware
flowing in filth to the sea
and felt your white beard waving
in the New Jersey dawn.
I paid to visit 431 Stevens Street
and paid to call your name
and paid to ride across your bridge
and paid for a cigar at your drug
and paid for a shirt at your department store
and paid for a can of soup at your Supermarket
and pissed in your restroom free.
Captain
you're a million dollar business
but all through Camden
I could not find
a copy of *The Leaves of Grass*.
They did not know who you were
in the slum section
under the Swedish roofs
nor cared to know
anything but the buck
and, dear poet of the American Way,
you gave them the American dream
you gave them the god of gods
you gave them the means
you gave them your name
you gave them a million dollar industry.
Oh, captain
what have we become
to use a name like Whitman
to sell the American Way?

. . . ANOTHER SEASON
for Pamela

autumn was our season
when we lay naked
in the warm suns of summer
watching the leaves fall calmly to earth
not feeling the coming frost of winter
nor the vultures of youth.
we sang our song
lying gayly upon the ground
smelling the fresh air
blowing through the pines
whistling in the oaks
and settling over our nude bodies.
we dreamed our dreams
and in our minds
saw them in reality
saw our passions as unending
and our love unconquerable.
yes, we were unyielding
in our childish ways
not willing to admit tomorrow
but we were young;
like giants, power
and strength were with us.
but autumn was a season
and seasons pass
as does youth
and dreams become dreams
and passion fades   .
like images lost in a mirror.
now you sing one song
and i another
and now we're dressed
in our garbs of different roles,
i, still dreaming
but, you, no longer a child.
time has no pains
only the thoughts
that come to life
in the stillness of a winter night.

OMYAH

Omyah, god of the forgotten
i saw the rain fall like fire
from the mushroom clouds
over bikini atoll
and seal the fate of a generation.
Omyah, god of the searching
i saw blind men stumble
in a city lost to darkness
trying to find their sight
yet found only the falling fragments
of angry wars that now are history.
Omyah, god of those who love
i saw a thirsty mob
look everywhere for water
and not find it
for they couldn't see over the lake.
i saw your wisdom
i felt your warmth
and i knew you were with us
on a journey toward fulfillment.
Omyah, god of the gentle
forgive those who cannot understand
the hollow trails they blaze
and help a young world
bring love to christianity.
Omyah, god
you're the lsd
we've searched for.

SHE

She read the *Reader's Digest*
and heard the mornin' news
yet she knew all there was to know
about us and a generation.

We walked easy around her
and spoke in silent whispers
kissed in darkened corners
and never talked of love
until it was too late.

But, at last
came the day of lights
and love fell on her eyes
you cried
and I walked out the door

the porch light dim.

WOMAN
for Jan

No object holds beauty for man
like the warm eyes of she
who would keep his soul in a
        tin can.
Bow in the mornin' sun to a goddess
cloaked in the fog
her face shinin' like a beacon light
callin' the fools to fall
        on knees
and worship the hem
of her mini-skirt
and the flesh showing above
        her nylons.
Oh, woman, I'd like to climb
inside your window
and sleep the night with you
and praise God's Trojan Horse
        to mankind.

JUDY WIXON

Oh you gods of
            long
            low
            lonely notes
let me hear your
            whine
in the deep blue-black of the night
when all peaceful souls rest.
Let me hear your whimpering woes
weave with my
            aloneness
in the deep blue-black of the night.
Let your mournful cries
mix with the night wind and
whisper how frightening the day
is when there are no arms to
close round the world and make
living seem full of happiness.

Oh you gods of
            long
            low
            lonely notes
soothe my aches and pains til he comes back.

DEDICATED TO MIKE

I want to
    hold a paintbrush
    as he does
and to
    slop the paint,
    creating colors
    symbolic of personalities
    only he knows,
    in a careless
    "I don't care" manner
yet in that manner
    originate
    colors, forms and
    meanings to
    Life
    the way he does.
I wish to love
    the smell and
    texture
    of clay
    as he does.
To form and
    mold
    the grey matter
    in order to
    express a
    complexity of
    his Self.
This I wish to do also.
And to take a pencil
    and from a piece of
    lead
    duplicate a breath
    of someone's
                    laughs from living
                    love for life
                    hate of hell
                    hope of heaven.

I wish . . .
I wish . . .

A little bird landed on
my shoulder
to whisper the
          Secrets of Life
into my ear —
but
    he relieved himself and
flew away
Now when anyone says
    "a little bird told me so"
I wonder
who
wiped the
    shit off his shoulder

CIVIL WAR HILLS

Trees in autumn
              turn your leaves
              blood red
    in memory of the
Civil War men.

Heffers
              when you decide to give milk
        give it blood red —
keeping the color of
the grass and soil
              that soaked up the red blood of
the men
    boys
who liked the color of
black walking free.

Red soil of the land
    raise the corn stalks to half mast
    water the crops with blood
              so they might grow with the
    desire
to feed the mouths of
    all people.

Civil War hills —
              bear the bones of men who
    love
a black and white polka-dotted country.

238

MELVIN WYMAN

DEATH OF A SALESMAN

Let's call this convention to order.
All the salesmen will kindly be seated.
The success of our group has been unprecedented
these past few years.
Wo've sold more of ourselves for less than
ever before in our history.
Congratulations.

Let's examine the record.
For only 15K a year you have managed
to keep the death factories operating,
you have cleverly traded a few charred
children for 2 cars in the garage,
you have acquired a color TV for the
bargain price of a pound of rotted flesh.
And it's only cost you your soul.
Congratulations.

If we continue marching onward with heads high,
with asses to the wind, we can sell more.
We do not have to stop with ourselves,
think of the price our unborn children will bring.
The market is free, the price is cheap.
Congratulate yourselves.

Remember, we are the true salesmen of the world,
eternity owes us what we have today.
All of the great sellouts have been one of us.
We don't ask much, just to be left alone
with the fruits of our sales, nothing more.
Our ranks are swelling, our recruiting is successful.
Congratulate ourselves.

Gentlemen, how much selling must we do,
before we're recognized for what we are?
When will the world understand us,
truly perceive what we are doing for mankind?
Not before they die, I trust.
Congratulate them.

COME

Come with me to
the
side
of
the
day

And let us grab a few
minutes for looking at yesterday.

So we may cry, having lost it
in such a careless way.

And at once try to regain it
for the days yet to come.

In darkness we go lightly
not seeing our way.

The soft dew
carressed blades of grass
and wept with pain.

Slices of time cut
me into ribbons of cement —
please step lightly.

Last winter several
trees shook their branches,
got up and left.